You Can 2

Life Lessons From My Mom's Untimely Death

Alvey Thompson, Jr

Author

You Can 2
Life Lessons From My Mom's Untimely Death

Author: Alvey Thompson, Jr

Publisher: YouCan2 Publishing

Copyright © 2021

ISBN: 978-1-946992-09-3

USD 19.95

First Edition: December 2021

To my mom, Vicki Warech.

Thank you for loving me unconditionally,
even when I did not reciprocate it.

Table of Contents

Acknowledgements

Creating this book has been a process of great love, healing, and growth. I have been fortunate to receive an extraordinary amount of love and support from many people. I am grateful for these amazing people and their contribution.

Pop, my grandfather, for showing me what unconditional love is and being my role-model growing up. Nan, my grandmother, for being the rock of our family. Thank you for your strength and love.

Alejandra Hernandez, my fiancé, for her love, generosity, kindness, open-mindedness, and passion for growth.

Paul Chek for his teachings, guidance, and authenticity. Michael Desanti for his leadership, guidance, and mentorship. Mo Hasan for coaching me during this book creation process and showing me how powerful presence and creation are in tandem.

The Acevedo family and the Moses family for supporting me and treating me like their own while I was a young boy growing up.

My close friends for their love, belief in me, and support.

My family for their unconditional love and always being there for me no matter what.

Foreword

As an NFL Pro Bowl wide receiver with the Miami Dolphins, College Head Football Coach, entrepreneur, philanthropist, and family man, I have a great appreciation for peak human performance. My associate and friend, Alvey "Danny" Thompson Jr, is dedicated and committed to making the world a better place, one person at a time. This shows in all areas of his life.

Over the past decade, Alvey has taught hundreds of athletes, business professionals, and other high performers how to optimize their holistic health in order to maximize their life. What makes him a great teacher is that he is a tremendous student, constantly learning and working to improve himself so that he can powerfully serve others. Over the past 10 years I have met countless current athletes, former athletes, and business professionals who could save themselves massive physical, mental, and emotional pain by following what Alvey teaches.

This book serves as an example of how much one can transform their lives by turning their pain into purpose. I love that Alvey is so open, vulnerable, and raw in sharing his transformational life lessons from his mom's untimely death. It feels as if Alvey is sitting next to you by the fireplace as he shares his most impactful stories and lessons with you.

-Chris Chambers

Preface

Why am I writing this book?

From my late twenties until my early thirties, I've been asked by many people how I can consistently be calm and grounded amongst all the chaos in the world. Most people who meet me assume my disposition has always been this way. This couldn't be farther from the truth.

As a coach, I have had the good fortune of working with countless professional athletes, business professionals, and entrepreneurs. Any yet, it seems like regardless of location or industry, my clients find themselves in the same predicament. They are yearning to improve their health, their relationships, or get clarity on what they desire their life to look like, but barely have a clue on where to start.

I remember being in this same place. What I found over the last 6 years, since my mom died, is that all the answers that I was looking for were already inside of me.

If you are seeking to improve the conditions in your life and do not know where to begin, allow this book to serve as a simple starting point. I'm confident that there are lessons from my personal growth journey that will resonate with where you are in your path.

Hi, I'm Alvey "Danny" Thompson Jr. aka Mr. YouCan2. First of all, thank you for choosing to read this book. I wrote it for a very specific reason: I keep getting asked how I transformed my life for the better. The way I grew from the trials and tribulations in my relationship with my mom shows that growth Is always available to us if we choose it.

This book serves three purposes. (1) To inspire you to stop doing the things in your life that are no longer serving you. (2) To start taking actions that will take you closer to where you desire to be in life. (3) To provide actionable ways that you can create the life of your dreams.

Introduction

Growing up, my mom, Vicki Warech, was my rock. As a single parent she did everything she could to ensure that my brother and I had a great life. Being a momma's boy during my youth, I was attached to her hip. Everywhere she would go, I would go. My mom provided me with everything I could have ever wanted as a child. I was so spoiled. She would spend money that she didn't have to make sure I had the equipment I needed for sports, all the in-style clothes for school, and the video game systems that were popular at the time.

Fast forwarded to my high school years, our relationship started to change drastically. My affinity for my mom decreased because of the way I viewed she was living her life and because of how I viewed my own life. This caused us to have a fraction of the loving relationship that I now know we could have had.

Why read this book?

Reviewing my own story, I can see how my mom's death was a catalyst to my personal growth journey. As crazy as it may sound, I don't think I would be the compassionate, caring, and loving person that I am now if my mom did not die the way she died. The way she died and the dynamics of our relationship at the time had me re-evaluate my life and decide to intentionally change for the better. Anyone who knew me from my teenage years can tell you that my personality has done a complete 180 when you compare it to where I am now. We laugh about it quite frequently. I was a wild boy (we'll save those stories for another book).

I am a firm believer that we are more similar than we are different. Based on that belief, I think there are certain life lessons that I have learned from my mom's death that may resonate with you. We all know what it feels like to be at our own version of rock bottom. Mine came at the age of 26 when my mom unexpectedly died. Take a moment to think about when you experienced your rock bottom. When this happened, did you rise out of it, or did you stay there longer than you would have liked?

This book serves as a real-life example of how I got to my rock bottom and eventually made my way out of it, growing into the best version of myself in the process. I am not perfect. My situation wasn't unique. I know that you and every other human being on this planet has what it takes to turn your trials and tribulations into triumph.

Each chapter is set up in the following way. First, I describe a pivotal story involving my mom and me. Second, I explain the transformational life lesson I learned based on this interaction. Third, I provide an example of how one of my clients used this lesson in their life to improve their own well-being. Finally, I leave you with a short summary of how you can apply this lesson to your life if you choose to do so.

While the stories are authentic, I have changed the names of all my clients.

The last thing I want to leave you with is this: Relationships with family can be complicated. I've found from personal experience that it is much easier to be compassionate with strangers and acquaintances than it is to our own family members. At the end of the day, most people are doing their best, especially the people you love most. As you read this book, think about the people who are closest to you. At any moment when you feel the desire to reach out to them or tell them that you love them, do it. Stop thinking that you will have the opportunity to do it later. You never know when your last opportunity will be.

Chapter 1: Start Within

"The most splendid achievement of all is the constant striving to surpass yourself and to be worthy of your own approval."

- Denis Waitley

It is a beautiful cool morning in Weston, Florida, in November of 2006. Weston is a very affluent suburb with mansions, luxurious homes, and people with significant wealth. My mom and I grew up in Bonaventure, Florida, which was nothing like Weston at all. Bonaventure had a few homes, small townhouses, and large families working to fit everybody into small spaces. This was not the same type of affluence that you saw in Weston. Bonaventure became a part of Weston in 1997, which is how the two of us ended up situated there at this time. Urban planning at its best, mixing the lower-middle class with the rich.

Growing up, my home always had problems. There were holes patched in the walls, stained tile floors, cracked cabinets, mold hidden in nearly every corner, and cockroaches for roommates. This night, however, was different. My mom and I had frantically been cleaning the house for the last three days because we had a special guest coming, the Head Coach for Georgetown University's football program, Kevin Kelly.

I was in my senior year of high school and had just completed my final varsity football season. As a team captain, I earned "honorable mention" for the county and was selected to play in the North vs. South Broward All-star game. It was during one of these practices at the all-star game where I played to my fullest potential. I had two sacks on the quarterback, two tackles for loss--wreaking havoc in the backfield. One of the highlights was a spectacular open-field tackle I made on a running back. This is an incredible feat for any player my size at 270 pounds trying to stop a person weighing 100 pounds less and much quicker, faster, and elusive.

After this practice, I was approached by a slightly oversized, tall white man named Luke Thompson. Coach Thompson was the linebackers coach for Georgetown University and visited the all-star game as the recruiter for the South Florida area. He came up to me with a big smile on his face and said, "Danny [the name I went by at the time], you are the exact type of defensive tackle that we are looking for at Georgetown."

My eyes got wide. I could not believe that I was having a conversation with and being recruited by a coach from the famous Georgetown University. Georgetown is one of the top 25 highest ranked institutions in the country and known as one of the best institutions worldwide. I was a great student and excelled at my sport, but never in my wildest imagination did I think I would have the opportunity to go to such a premier institution.

Georgetown University serves as the iconic and historic landmark perched upon the hilltop of northwest Washington, DC, one of the most culturally diverse places in the world. It is considered the international capital of the world, global housing headquarters for organizations such as the World Bank Group and Danaher. I couldn't believe that I might have the opportunity to call Washington, DC, my playground. Up until that point, I was getting recruited by other schools in the Patriot League, the same league that Georgetown football was in, most notably Colgate University and Lafayette College. Both schools looked great on paper. They are both tremendous academic institutions. They both win a lot of football games and consistently compete for the championship every year. The only problem is they're both in the middle of nowhere and have harsh winters, which sounded like a death sentence to my happiness.

Being from South Florida, I am accustomed to beautiful beaches, city life, and diverse cultures around every corner. I was instantly turned off after discovering that Colgate and Lafayette were located in Hamilton, NY, and Easton, PA, respectively. When the coach from Colgate was recruiting me, he was all excited to tell me how their campus just got a massive upgrade that all the students were raving about, a new movie theater on campus. I had to hold back my laughter. I chuckled to myself, "A movie theater?" It's going to take way more than that to get me excited to go to Colgate. Their campus seemed dull and cold, way too cold. Blistering cold! In my mind, as an 18-year-old, if it dipped under 70 degrees, you knew my hoodie and sweatpants were coming on. So, when I heard that Georgetown was going to be in the picture, I was ecstatic. DC has all four seasons with its mid-Atlantic positioning, but winters were not nearly like those in the northeast.

Fast forward a couple of days later, and I'm sitting on my couch inside my house, not a cockroach insight. The home was sparkling clean. There was no slight sense of mildew coming from the bathroom. We had done what many people do when special people come over-- clean like our lives depend on it because it potentially did. I was preparing for the most significant moment of my life —the doorbell rings. I feel the butterflies in my stomach. I nervously dust off my favorite black Ralph Lauren polo with the matching Girbaud shorts and Jordan Eights, my best sneakers. I stand up, take a deep breath, walk down to the now sparkling hallway floor, pass the kitchen, and make one final inspection to make sure no cockroaches are rolling by to ruin my life. I turn the doorknob anxiously, open the door, and there stands the man that potentially holds the keys to my future. Coach Kevin Kelly, the head football coach of Georgetown University, had now entered my home.

I shake his hand. He shakes my mom's hand, and we make our way back to the living room. After exchanging some pleasantries, Coach Kelly gets right down to business. He said, "Danny, you are exactly the type of player that I'm looking for here at Georgetown. You're a great athlete, an excellent student, and an outstanding young man. I'm very impressed by your film and how you play the game. Coach Thompson says you're an excellent individual. I want you to come in and be one of a handful of players to help turn this program around. (Georgetown went 2-9 in 2006). When you go to Georgetown, you're part of an amazing network. By going here, you are potentially setting yourself up for life in any industry that you can think of. Whether it's law, finance, business, entrepreneurship, you name it. We have alumni in the football program, who will be able to take care of you and make sure that you're put in a position to succeed. I want to offer you a scholarship to this program and be a part of this change. What do you say?"

For a moment, I was speechless. On the inside, my heart is pounding, my palms are sweaty, ["knees weak, arms are heavy vomit on his sweater already, Mom's spaghetti" – Eminem] and I am tingling with joy. But on the outside, I played it cool, trying to hide my ecstatic glee. "Coach, thank you so much. I'm so honored and humbled by this opportunity. I want to give it some time and talk it over with my mom to make sure that we make the best decision for me."

Coach Kelly replied, "I completely understand that. Take your time. I'm looking forward to hearing back from you soon." We all get up from the couch, walk over to the door, and say our goodbyes. As Coach Kelly walks away, I shut the door behind him and yell out, "YES!"

I could not believe that I was getting the opportunity to go to Georgetown. I was going to one of the best schools in the world, in the international capital of the world, and being a part of an up-and-coming football program. I would get the opportunity to walk the same hallways as some of the most amazing athletes of all time, with Allen Iverson, Alonzo Mourning, Patrick Ewing, and Dikembe Mutombo, to name a few legends I watched growing up. Everything that I had dreamed of was going to be coming true.

I look at my mom, and she is smiling from ear to ear. Her eyes are wide open. She is glowing. She has an energy and vitality that I had never seen from her before. My mom had struggled with her health my entire life. A few of her conditions included obesity, type two diabetes, high blood pressure, heart problems, addiction to opioid medications, and an overall sense of cloudiness in her health outlook.

My entire life consisted of her constantly feeling sick, tired, always being in bed, and not taking care of herself genuinely. By my senior year of high school, I saw my mom get picked up by the ambulance five times. The sirens would blast throughout my small neighborhood, having all of our neighbors rush outside to investigate the emergency at hand. But at this moment, she had a sparkle in her eye. I thought to myself, "Wow! If my going to Georgetown could give her this type of energy, I can only imagine the types of things I can do that will finally improve her health. My mom's poor health has weighed heavily on my heart ever since I was a young boy. Seeing how this scholarship offer lit her up, I figured my accomplishments moving forward would ultimately allow her to heal.

Fast forward nine months, I'm in the car with my mom, driving east on Interstate 595 heading towards Fort Lauderdale Airport because my Georgetown career starts the next day in DC. About 15 minutes into the trip, I feel this tightness in my heart. An immense pressure builds up in the middle of my face. I don't know what this emotion is, and before I know it, I start crying—really crying—crying in a way that I have not called before. At that moment, I realized for the first time exactly how much I was going to miss my mom, close friends, and being in south Florida.

It dawned on me these last nine months that I was excited about going to Georgetown, But I wasn't excited for me. I was excited about the optics of going to such a fantastic university. I knew how much my mom would brag about her football player star son to her friends and family. I learned how proud my family was of me. I knew how proud my friends were of me. I was happy to have their approval.

It wasn't until my face was covered in tears that I realized that I wasn't going to Georgetown for me at all. I wasn't excited for me. The thought of going there now scared me because I wasn't doing it for the one person that it mattered for. I was doing it for my mom. I thought if I could make her happy, I could help her get healthy. I was doing this for how good it looked to be one of three players on my high school football team to be receiving a Division I scholarship and playing at the Division I college level—knowing that less than 2% of high school football players go on to play Division I college football. I loved how proud people that weren't even close to me were excited to tell someone they knew someone going to Georgetown.

The apple doesn't fall far from the tree. My entire life, my mom's validation was always based on what other people were saying to her. My mom would give money that she didn't have to other people in exchange for their appreciation and gratitude. But my mom didn't have that same appreciation for herself. It was quite the opposite. Nothing that she did was ever for her. It was always to look good for others. At that moment, I got the same sense of external validation from my mom. At that time, both of us were the type of people who wanted everyone else to tell us how good we were doing, how much we were helping them, how much they liked us, how much we were of service, and ultimately how we were making their lives better. But at that time, I never really congratulated myself on my accomplishments.

I never truly appreciated myself for what I was accomplishing. This also applied to my mom. She only felt validated when someone else was telling her how great of a job she was doing. When someone else was saying, "Thank you, Vicki! I couldn't have done this without you!" That is the only time that she felt worthy and whole.

The first lesson I am sharing with you is this: validation must come from the inside. Internal validation exceeds external validation in every way possible. In a situation where I'm waiting for someone else's approval, I will never indeed be satisfied or fulfilled. I am giving someone else my power. I am allowing someone else's words to decide how I feel about myself.

I've realized this way of being doesn't serve me. Now, I have shifted my mindset to make sure I'm my biggest cheerleader every time I do something. I make sure that I am celebrating myself every day on the things I am achieving in life to build momentum within me. It makes a deposit in my heart and soul that I know that I am capable and worthy of any and every single thing that I am doing in my life. I work to teach my clients the same thing.

I had a client named Eric, who, when we first started working together, did not realize how much he was waiting for someone to affirm him, to make him feel like he was worthy or capable of creating certain things in his life. Whenever he wasn't being affirmed, he was questioning himself, wondering "what if?", overthinking, and most of all, he wasn't taking action in his life in the direction he truly wanted. He didn't even see this happening in front of his own eyes every day. Before it finally clicked for him, he would wait to get the approval of a family member, a friend, or a co-worker so he could find value within himself. Once he discovered this was happening in his life, he was able to take a step back and soon realized that his power had been yielded to someone else.

With this new awareness, he has committed to regaining his power. He found that the most important and effective way for him to do that is by validating himself. Every single night, he counts his wins, no matter how big or small. He takes the time to acknowledge the successes that he had that day. Every time he noted that win, it built up a reservoir of more and more confidence in himself. He uses that confidence to take courageous action in every aspect of his life. That was important to him. Today, I'm proud to say that Eric is now the type of person who knows what he is capable of, appreciates himself, and takes consistent action in his life because he validates himself every day—never waiting for someone else to do it for him.

What You Can Stop Doing

Stop relying on other people's words, feelings, and approval to validate how you feel about yourself.

 What You Can Start Doing

Validate yourself based on your ethics (the agreements you make with yourself).

 How You Can 2

Create your ethics. What are the agreements that you will make with yourself on how you desire to live your life? Honor these agreements consistently. Take time to acknowledge and appreciate yourself daily by writing down your wins for the day.

Chapter 2: Martyr Complex

"Don't sacrifice yourself too much, because if you
sacrifice too much there's nothing else you can give,
and nobody will care for you."
- Karl Lagerfeld

It's May of 2015. I returned from the best trip of my life, having spent the last week with two of my best friends, Shabazz and Travis, on vacation in Abu Dhabi and Dubai. At this point in my life, I was 26-years-old and worked so hard to establish myself as a high-quality personal trainer, sports performance coach, and nutrition coach for a few years now. This was the beginning stage of my entrepreneurial journey and doing the work that truly set my soul on fire. I was helping people become the best versions of themselves through eating, moving, and feeling the best they could.

While we were in Dubai, we were living lavishly. We were going to six-star hotels, eating fantastic food, pulling up to extravagant parties, visiting beautiful artificial beaches, and experiencing culture, unlike anything I'd seen before. Being relatively early in my entrepreneurship journey, I wasn't making nearly enough money to afford to go on a trip like this. Still, my friend Shabazz called me randomly on Christmas Eve, the year before, in 2014. He said, "Yo Danny! You are not going to believe this! I found these tickets online to go to either Abu Dhabi, Hong Kong or South Africa for about $200. I don't know what the date would be for the trip at that price, but I wanted to see if you want to take this leap of faith?" Astonished, I replied, "Bro, whatever you find, whatever place you decide, whatever the date is, book it and I'll be there."

Fast forward six months to May, we ended up having the time of our lives. After our week abroad, we flew back stateside. On my last night in New York City, I decided to go out and meet up with some of my fraternity chapter brothers who lived in the area. Whenever the Delta Theta chapter of Omega Psi Phi Fraternity is in town, we make sure to get together and fellowship.

A few hours into partying, we were all outside getting ready to hit the next bar when I suddenly felt my phone vibrating in my pocket. I grabbed my phone, pulled it out, looked down, and checked to see who was calling me. It was my grandmother. Mind you, my grandmother never calls me, let alone at 11:30 PM. Anxiety started to fill my body from head to toes. Something was very wrong. My heart started racing. My throat started to constrict. Sweat began to pour down my entire body. At this moment, I didn't have the courage or the strength to answer the phone. Because I had so many friends around me, I could not take the risk of having a physical, mental, and emotional breakdown in front of them. I put my phone back in my pocket, let it ring away, and continued to drink and party into the night.

Around 1 AM, I decided I had enough fun for one night and said my goodbyes to my chapter brothers Jon, Danny, and Aaron. What felt like the longest subway ride from Brooklyn back to Harlem awaited me. The entire ride back to Shabazz's place, all I could think about was the worst-case scenario. Right when I got off the subway, I decided to face that call. It was late, so I knew my grandmother was asleep. So, I decided to call my uncle, Scott, instead. It seemed like the phone rang for an eternity. Waiting and waiting and waiting for him to answer, but to no avail.

Thinking about who else could know what was going on, I decided to call my brother, Hank. Hank picked up the phone crying hysterically, "Mom's not going to make it! Mom's not going to make it. They're saying mom's not going to make it." Never in my 26 years of life up to that point have I ever heard my brother wail like that. Immediately, my heart began to sink. Tears started to fill my face, and I was now crying with him because I got the gut-wrenching news that my mom wouldn't make it out of the coma that she was in.

This was the most challenging moment of my entire life. My brother is a big believer in God. The whole time my mom was in this condition, he kept insisting, "God won't let mom die. God won't let mom die. God won't let mom die." Mom still died. Up to that point, my brother never thought that this was a real possibility. He ignored it the whole time, using prayer as a crutch to help him numb out the thought that our mom could pass away any day now.

On the other hand, I had seen the writing on the wall. For a long time, my mom never filled her cup. For much of her life that I witnessed, she rarely focused on what was in her control, in terms of how she was eating, how she was moving, how she was managing her stress, managing her emotions, doing things that were fun for her, or anything else to help improve her health. She had many scares in the hospitals before. She had been picked up by the ambulance at my home many times before. She had escaped death before. When my mom was placed in this coma, I sensed that something was different. I didn't think she would make it out of this one, but I never fully admitted it. I guess we were both experiencing our version of denial.

In my mind, I had prepared myself for this moment. But when I got the news from my brother, it was like I knew that a piece of me was lost forever. We cried hysterically together on that dreadful phone call. Sadness, anger, pain, and shock ran through my entire being. To know that I was never going to see my mom again destroyed me. My brother and I eventually hung up the phone, both of us still in tears. Instantly, I decided to call my dad.

My dad, Alvey Sr., was not there for much of my life. He did not raise me; my mom did. They had a falling out when I was three-years-old. He moved to Atlanta to live with his brother. He would call me on my birthday, send me $100 as a gift, and that was about it. That was the extent of our relationship until I reached the fifth grade. He and my mom reconciled, so he moved back in with us for a few years before being kicked out again, moving to Miami to live with my other grandmother. We didn't have a bad relationship. There was no malice; I wasn't mad at him. He wasn't mad at me. We have some similar personality traits where it can be easy to let time go by without reaching out to people. We could go months without speaking yet still have a relationship where we loved each other. This allowed us to keep in touch from time to time.

I called my dad. After a few rings, he picks up the phone. With tears in my eyes and sorrow in my voice, I told him, "My mom is not going to make it. We are pulling the plug." At that moment, my dad started to cry. Up to that point in my life, I had never heard my dad call. EVER! For him to be crying after he heard from me, his baby boy, that my mom wasn't going to make it, I knew it hurt him deeply. I knew it hit him hard. My dad was never one to show emotions. He was highly stoic. Never too high, never too low. We talked for a little bit, but very few words were spoken, consistent with most of our conversations.

Eventually, we say our goodbyes. I made it a point to tell him how much I loved him. Losing my mom created a greater sense of gratitude for my dad being alive. We hung up.

Walking back from the subway station to Shabazz's apartment, I was filled with despair and shame. It was like a black could be surrounding my entire body from the inside out. With my soul shattered, body slumping, I knocked on Shabazz's door. He opened it to find me bawling my eyes out. My shirt was soaked from a mixture of sweat and tears. He's looking at me in total shock. "Yo! What happened? What's good? What's going on?" The only words I could muster up were, "My mom's not going to make it." I buried my face into my hands. He looked at me, so surprised because he had no idea what I was talking about.

At the time, my mom had already been in the hospital in that coma for about ten weeks. However, I didn't tell anybody. Only a couple of family friends and immediate family knew, but I wasn't telling anybody what was happening in my circle. On the outside, everything looked great. My career was thriving. My new business was growing. I had lost about 30 pounds. My skin was clear. My vibe was different. My energy was up. Yet, I was holding all my pain inside.

I told Shabazz that my mom was dying and that she had been in the hospital for these last ten weeks, and I hadn't told anyone about it. In my mind, I didn't want to put any pressure on anybody else or bring anyone else's mood down on account of what I was going through. Shabazz held space for me. He sat there with me; he listened to me; he hugged me. He did what great friends do. To this day, I'm so grateful that he could be there for me in that type of way. It showed me how special our friendship is.

After fully expressing what was going on in my life and all the pain I was experiencing, I went to sleep. The following day, I flew back to Fort Lauderdale. From there, I went to my apartment in Plantation, threw my stuff down, and dashed to the hospital. The hospital called me to finalize everything. When I arrived, I nervously walked up to the sliding glass doors, silently went up the elevator with my head slumped down, and went in to sign paperwork. The nurse asked me, "Do you want to see your mom one last time?" For whatever reason, I said yes. She escorted me into the small dark room where they had moved my mom to. The nurse removed the sheet, and there laid my lifeless mother. As I looked at her, I couldn't believe that this had happened. Her body was there, but all life had escaped. The finality of this moment paralyzed me. It finally hit me that I was never going to be with my mom again physically. The most important person in my life was gone forever. I felt broken.

At that time, she and I used to argue all the time. We didn't have a good relationship. We weren't close. It's so silly when I look back at it because I was so petty to her. I literally wouldn't let her be my friend on Facebook. That's how shitty I was to her at that time. This whole time I wanted her to work on her health, and I wanted her to be better. She started making some changes to her lifestyle the last few months, but it was too late. All before that time, she would do anything in her power to help fill somebody else's cup, but she wouldn't fill up her own. She wouldn't fill up her cup by eating well. She wouldn't fill up her cup by constantly moving and exercising. She wouldn't fill up her cup by managing her stress. She wouldn't fill up her cup by doing things that excited her. She wouldn't fill up her cup by going out and living a fulfilling life.

Instead, she would do anything for somebody else to eat better and be able to move better. She would hold the space so someone else could vent and manage their stress. She would give other people money that she didn't have to be happy or feel safe. This was a huge frustration of mine as an adult. At this age, I was in a position where I was old enough to understand that my mom wasn't doing things to take care of herself. Instead, she was doing all these things for everybody else. So many fights and our arguments stemmed from me telling her not to do something for me and instead do it for herself. To not spend money on friends and family that she did not have.

Unfortunately, my words never landed. They never stuck. When I left the hospital that day, I realized that something had to change within me. I learned how I was showing up in the world, for myself, my friends, and my family, all got to change. Going and visiting my mom and seeing her lifeless body, feeling the pain, the agony, the struggle within myself to see how I also contributed to that ate me alive. It showed me that I had to make considerable changes to my life.

My biggest lesson from that day is how important it is to fill my cup up first. I get to make sure that I'm doing everything within my power to be as physically, emotionally, mentally, and spiritually healthy as possible. I get to help myself as much as I can to go out there and help others truly. My nutrition was raised to a higher level; my training leveled up, my development journey became a priority. All my actions from that day forward were made to become the best me possible because I saw how my mom never did that. Most of her actions came from an empty place where she would try to give and give and give without ever having the physical, mental, or emotional resources to do so effectively. That vacant place ultimately killed her.

One of the clients I work with, named Erin, reminded me so much of my mom. Erin would do anything for her kids, her husband, and her friends to ensure that they were good. She consistently sacrificed her time, joy, passions, and overall mental and emotional health to serve those around her. It was reminiscent of the shadow side of the mother archetype, focused on taking care of others and being a martyr, if that's what is required. As a result, Erin's health was tanking. She was miserable. She was sad. She gained weight. She wasn't eating well at all. Yet, she was doing everything in her power to help all the people in her life that she loved. What was missing for her was doing all those things in a way that allowed her to do it from a full cup. There was a lack of awareness around how her current actions were not sustainable because she was slowly running herself into the ground. If nothing changed, there was a good chance that she could end up with the same fate as my mom. How could she be there for her kids, husband, friends, and family if she was no longer physically there to help?

Erin initially came to work with me because she wanted to lose 25 pounds that she gained due to being overstressed and trying to do everything for everyone. She sacrificed her nutrition, hydration, movement, and rest in the process. After some deep digging and uncomfortable conversations, she started to realize how much she was self-sabotaging.

It was amazing to see her come to her conclusions based on our conversations. She discovered her limiting belief that she had to do things for everyone else before doing them herself. This was backward because to powerfully serve her kids, husband, friends, and family; she would need to have the energy required to do it.

She shared how the headaches and joint pain she woke up with daily negatively impacted her ability to connect with her loved ones. To fix the headaches and joint pain, we co-created a plan that addressed her needs for proper sleep, relaxation, nutrition, hydration, and movement. We worked on her thinking, building awareness around how specific thoughts triggered her. Then we created a system for working with those thoughts to allow her to focus on getting her the results she wanted.

She was reframing her life to put herself first before putting all these people before her didn't change at the snap of a finger. But every single day, she set out to do one thing for herself. That one thing turned into two. Those two eventually turned into ten. Now she's living a life that she's proud of, and that's fulfilling. She has impressive confidence where she courageously takes action in her life and helps those around her at an even higher level. Filling her cup is now a non-negotiable for her. With everything that's overflowing from her cup, she can powerfully serve and give to all of those around her.

Chapter 3: 360 Health

"Health is a complete state of complete harmony of the body mind and spirit. When one is free from physical disabilities and mental distractions, the gates of the soul open."

- B.K.S Iyengar

It's the Summer of 2013. It's a hot, humid, and rainy South Florida day. Like many days throughout the week, I heard an argument happening in my mom's room. Accustomed to these encounters, I chilled for a minute, tried to collect my thoughts, and did my best to ignore them. While the argument was going on for what felt like hours, I finally came out of my room and moved towards the discussion. My brother slammed his door shut. Annoyed, I looked at my mom and asked her, "What's going on? What's wrong?" With the tone of a victim, she miserably explained, "Nobody cares about me! No one appreciates me!"

My mom was going on and on about how nobody honestly cares about her or truly respects her. It speaks directly to the external validation I explained earlier. I could see my mom going back into this familiar pattern. Suddenly, she brought me up into it. Mind you, at this point in 2013, my mom and I would argue all the time. At the core of most of those arguments was my displeasure with her trying to do things for me.

At this point of my life, I was a disgruntled 23-years-old who was used to living on my own because I lived on my own for four years at Georgetown but was now living with my mom. Deep down, I was so angry about this, regularly questioning myself, "Why am I 23-years-old, still living at my mom's house?" My viewpoint on this created self-doubt, unworthiness, and frustration within me. This mindset caused a significant amount of resentment that I had towards my mom.

That irritation was towards me, but I would redirect it towards my mom because I did not have the tools to take ownership of it. This resulted in countless arguments on how I didn't need her help, even though she always wanted to provide it. She often wanted to cook food for me. She would take her time to cook a delicious meal for me, which would piss me off. Every week she would take the time to wash my clothes, dry them, fold them, and place them on my bed. When I found my clothes folded on my bed, I'd be livid.

This was all a result of the story I was telling myself in my head. In this story I created, every time my mom did something for me, it somehow stunted my growth. These thoughts were rooted in my insecurities. I can see that I was so caught up in my opposing viewpoint of what it meant for me to live at home and have my mom do all these things for me. As a result, I frequently held this against her instead of taking responsibility for my reality.

When I was in her room that summer day in 2013 after she had just got done having an argument with my brother, my mom and I got into a heated exchange. She screamed, "You are so ungrateful! All I do is make your life easier!" I yelled back in defense, "I don't need you to do anything for me! I don't want you to do anything for me!" Hurt by the fact that I did not want her to support me in any way, she replied, "Why don't you appreciate me? Why don't you let me help you? So many people wish they could get this help from their mom!" I was so angry. We're going back and forth, saying mean things to each other. Then out of nowhere, she shouted, "I wish I was dead!"

Blood was boiling in my body. I turned around behind me and swung an overhand right as hard as I could into the wall that separates the kitchen from the dining room. Half of my forearm went crashing through the wall, crumbling the drywall behind it. I pull my arm out and see a large, deep gash on my fist. In shock, I stared at my balled-up fist, realizing that as I punched the wall, I narrowly missed squarely hitting the metal beam structure in the wall by two inches, deeply scratching my hand in the process; If I had squarely hit that piece of steel, I would have indeed shattered my right hand.

But that didn't matter to me. I was infuriated. At this moment, I made a profound realization: My mom's way of life proved to me that she did not want to be alive. Since I was in high school, deep within me, I felt something off with the way my mom lived her life. However, I could never quite put my finger on what it was. But now, it was crystal clear. Her lifestyle was slowly killing her. [this sentence can be better. It's a powerful message and not written with a punch] She never exercised, rarely moved, and consistently ate processed foods. Every meal consisted of some combination of fast food, takeout, or TV dinners. That's how we grew up. That was the same way I ate until just six months before this argument.

At this age, I started to invest in my health physically, consciously eating better. My diet consisted of whole foods: meat, veggies, fruits, real stuff that came from the earth and grew from the world. My training regimen was on point, working out six days a week, spending one to two hours in the gym, playing basketball, being active. In my estimation, my health was in a good place based on the actions I took with my nutrition and movement. My mom's life was the opposite. The fact that she could express that she no longer wanted to live hurt me deep down in my soul because at that moment, I believed she truly meant it.

I've realized that when a person is sick when in pain, they will say and do some of the worst things on this earth. I know because I've exemplified this myself. My mom and my brother were also great examples of how this manifests. When she told me she no longer wanted to be alive, there was a piece of me that believed her. Granted, I think she said it because she was upset, but there was truth in her words. The pain of feeling underappreciated, lacking a personal vision, eating horribly, not moving, addiction, not getting outside in nature, and a victim mentality contributed to her negative emotions. But a natural part of me genuinely believed, based on all the actions I had seen up to that point, that she had reached a tipping end. As a result, she didn't want to be alive.

The way she would travel around our small home was a reminder of this. She was using a wheelchair or a walker to move twenty feet at a time. My mom would go through the cycle of using the wheelchair to get from her room to the kitchen to the bathroom daily. I saw her make that path for the majority of my life. She was seeing this now, as a 23-year-old, and hearing that she no longer wanted to be alive pushed me over the edge.

When I hit that wall, not only did I realize how much her words hurt me, but I can look back now, and I can see why those words hurt me so much. At that time, I thought health was only a physical thing. Health meant going to the gym. Health meant going for walks. Health was nutrition, as in how well you're eating. That was my very simplified and limited view of health. What I realized during that interaction is that health is so much more than just the physical side of it.

Not only was my mom unhealthy physically. She was severely unwell emotionally, mentally, and spiritually. She consistently experienced emotional lows, with a few highs sprinkled in. The lows were so low that it would have her say horrific things about herself, her family, and the people she loved. It's so clear to me now that I also had poor emotional health. Yes, I was working out. Yes, I was eating better. But when I got mad, I was ready to explode. This would manifest into screaming matches with my mom, fights with my brother, and being prepared to fight strangers on a drunken weekend night. All because I did not know how to handle my emotions. Emotional intelligence evaded me for the entirety of my early to mid-twenties.

We also suffered mentally. My mom's mental health was, gosh, nonexistent. All her traumas, the pain that she'd been through, her victim mentality, her fixed mindset, and many of the prescription opioid drugs she had taken for decades deteriorated her mental health. It showed up in the way she self-sabotaged. It showed up in her actions. It showed up in how she spoke to and yelled at the people that she loved the most. The things that I heard her say to my brother are unforgettable. They break my heart when I think about them today. They're haunting words that I should have never been saying.

I was no Zen master myself. My mental health was erratic. My unrealistic, personal expectations of where I thought I was supposed to be as a twenty-three-year-old who graduated from Georgetown University made me insecure and angry. There were so many things that I thought I was going to be doing upon graduation that I wasn't. As a result, I consistently beat myself up, using negative self-talk, formed ineffective habits, self-sabotaged, and kept myself small. During this time, I never fully lived to my potential because I treated myself and how I thought of myself.

My mom and I both lacked spiritual health. We were never religious growing up. I'm Jewish, culturally, because my mom is Jewish. But we didn't practice or celebrate any of the traditions. My dad's side of the family was Catholic. We did not go to church or practice any of those traditions either. What made us even remotely Catholic was celebrating Christmas and celebrating Easter. By observing, I mean exchanging gifts and eating food. It was never really to celebrate the true meanings of those holidays.

At the time, neither one of us had any spiritual connection. Neither one of us was connected to something bigger than ourselves. I didn't practice slowing down, meditating, practicing mindfulness, saying affirmations, utilizing visualization, or praying. I didn't have any tools that enabled me to practice presence, gratitude, or stillness. My mom didn't have any of those tools either. My mom's health wasn't where it could have been and how she deteriorated health negatively impacted her life. At that time, in 2013, I thought I had all aspects of my health dialed in. The sad truth is that neither one of us was healthy.

To achieve optimal health, one must consistently and intentionally work on health: physical, emotional, mental, and spiritual. Each pillar of health works synergistically with all the others, meaning that the combined effects of working on all of them are more significant than if you work on each of them individually.

In many societies, physical health is the most common pillar to work on. There are countless gyms, diet plans, and marketing telling you how to get in the best shape of your life if you follow their dream. Physical health is the most tangible form of health because many people decide to start on in their health journey. Some of the first questions people ask themselves are:

"How am I eating?"

"How am I moving?"

"How am I hydrating?"

"How am I mobilizing?"

How am I stretching?"

These are all great questions to ask, but it is only one piece of the puzzle.

In addition to physical health, it is so essential to pay love and attention to emotional health. Emotions are energy in motion experienced by you. They often appear as visceral feelings throughout the body, whether it is constriction of the throat, increased heart rate, butterflies in the stomach, nausea, or something else. Some questions to ask yourself when it comes to emotional health are:

"How am I working with my energy?"

"What is triggering me?"

"How am I breathing?"

"How am I managing my emotions and allowing that energy to continue to move?"

The extent to which you can manage your emotions dictates how robust your emotional health is. Consistently working on your emotional health has two significant benefits. First, it increases your emotional intelligence. Emotional intelligence is your ability to recognize, understand, and manage your own emotions. It also allows you to understand, identify, and influence the feelings of others.

This shows up in my life often today. When something triggers me, I now take the time to pause and recognize the event that triggered me. From there, I check in with myself to see what emotions I am feeling. Then I ask myself, "What values of mine are being challenged here that are causing these emotions?" Once I'm clear on that, I focus on taking action. That may show up in me communicating with a person involved in the triggering event. It may require me to have some alone time to meditate. It may show up in taking the energy I'm feeling and transmuting it into a workout. Or I may realize that I have no control over the situation and decide to release my attachment to it completely. It's all about using the tool that will allow me to move forward with a sense of peace in my life.

The second benefit is that it increases emotional resilience. Emotional resilience refers to your ability to adapt to stressful situations or crises. The beauty of emotional stability is that it does not necessarily change the world around you, but it changes how you interpret it. No shortage of chaos may be going on around me in my life these days. The difference in my level of emotional resilience has increased. This enables me to stay calm within the many storms of life. As a result, I make better decisions that positively impact myself and those around me. Both tools are critical when facing real-life situations under pressure, which inevitably, we all face in life.

Mental health focuses on working with everything happening between our ears, in our heads, and our minds It is a product of our psychological and cognitive well-being. Ultimately, the way you think will impact the words you use and the actions you take in your life. Some questions to ask yourself regarding building awareness around your mental health are:

"How am I working with my thoughts?"

"How am I distinguishing facts from my interpretations of the facts?"

"How am I thinking about myself?"

"Am I identifying every thought I have as being true or who I am?

Spiritual health can mean a variety of things to different people. I define spiritual health by taking responsibility for what I am creating in my life from moment to moment. It is a catalyst for my personal and spiritual growth, allowing me to reach my highest potential. Here are some questions to ponder regarding your spiritual health:

"How am I staying connected to something bigger than what is obvious to me?"

"What practices am I adhering to that allow me to connect with myself?"

"How often am I meditating?"

"Am I connecting to nature?"

"Do I believe in something bigger than myself?"

These four pillars of health give us the energy, vitality, and power to live to our highest potential. Living a fulfilling life starts and ends with the level of wellness we have physically, emotionally, mentally and spiritually. All of them require our love and attention. This is a foundational point that I drive home with my clients, no matter their individual goals.

One of my clients, Peter, is a perfect example of what happens when a person focuses on implementing a holistic approach to health. Peter was very much how I was back in 2013 when he first came to me in 2017. He told me he wanted to work on his health. We had deep conversations to unpack where his life currently was at that moment. Together, we combed carefully through his health and lifestyle questionnaires. Based on his answers, we discovered that his definition of health revolved around exercising a certain way and eating a certain way. His description of being healthy was limited at best. He was confusing being healthy with being fit. Being fit is defined as being able to do a specific task: i.e., lift a certain amount of weight, run a specific distance in a certain time, or look a certain way, aesthetically. While all those things are important, those are only pieces to the puzzle.

As Peter and I worked together, we had essential conversations on whether he was open to growing his healthy idea. With his approval, we started the intake process and dove deep into where he perceived himself to be in all aspects of his life:

Career and finances

Health / wellness / fitness

Personal relationship

Relationship with family and friends

Leisure time

Spiritual growth

Community involvement

We had an open, honest, and vulnerable conversation about each pillar in depth. As we peeled back the layers, he started to realize that there were holes, not just in his health, wellness and fitness, but in most areas of his life. Many of which he wasn't even aware of before working together. These holes included a strained relationship with his wife, stagnation in his business, a lack of quality sleep and recovery, and no time spent on his hobbies. All of which contributed to his high-stress levels that negatively impacted his health.

As we dove deeper into his goals, he realized that he wanted to achieve his fitness but was not limited to only his physical health and wellness. He began to take actionable steps in each domain of his life. He dedicated a specific time each day to be present with his wife. They started to have conversations on where they wanted to take the relationship and how they could get there. New commitments were made between the two of them, renewing the spark in their marriage. Simply creating the time to be present with her allowed her to feel seen and heard for the first time in years. This immediately brought them closer together.

Peter realized that the stagnation in his business came from his need control every little detail of his business. After an extensive conversation on the subject, he realized that he had issues trusting that his employees could do the higher-level work he consistently found himself holding onto. Because he was neck-deep in the day-to-day whirlwind of his business, he was not creating time to work on growing the business. By distinguishing what was in his control and his stories around why he could not trust others, Peter created space for himself to delegate work. Taking work off his plate made peace within him, allowed him to slow his inner world down, and ultimately allowed him to work on growing his business, which he did.

The most significant catalyst to Peter's growth was his dedication to being intentional with his time. Before working together, he was not intentional about making time for stillness, which caused most of the stress in his life. Instead of taking time to slow down and replenish his energy, he was burning from both ends of the candle. Incorporating practices like getting to bed by 10:30 PM consistently each night, taking breathing breaks during his workday, and utilizing meditation allowed him to have the energy to perform at a high level daily.

As that momentum started to build up, he started to build more confidence. He started to become more fulfilled. By consistently putting in the work, he noticed massive shifts in all aspects of his life. He's happier, fulfilled, and has more energy. He has great relationships at home and the office. He has a body that he's proud of. He realizes that health is more than just physical He became healthy when he focused on his physical, emotional, mental, and spiritual well-being. Now he utilizes these 360 approaches to health to ensure that he lives his life to the fullest. Whenever he feels like something is even slightly off in his life, he checks in to see every aspect of his health. Then he focuses on intentionally taking care of whichever pillar requires work, re-centering himself in the process.

What You Can Stop Doing

Stop limiting your definition of health to only your physical body.

 What You Can Start Doing

Realize that your health is holistic, meaning that there are physical, emotional, mental, and spiritual components that all work together.

 How You Can 2

Start building holistic health practices that work for you. This can include but is not limited to focusing on ways to optimize your nutrition, hydration, sleep/rest, thinking, moving, and breathing. Be intentional with your stress-management techniques, eating whole foods, time for introspection, and exercise. Sustainably do these, meaning you can do it daily without it feeling burdensome . These practices should energize you!

Count your WINS

Chapter 4: You Need Yourself

"Love yourself first and everything else falls into line."
- Lucille Ball

It was a late Saturday night in the Fall of 2012. My friends and I were hanging out, laughing, and enjoying ourselves after a fun night out. My phone started vibrating; I reached into my pocket, opened it up, and saw a lengthy text message from my mom. "Danny, why haven't I heard from you? I don't know why you're not talking to me. I didn't even do anything. This is unacceptable! I'm your mom. You should never do this to me! You shouldn't do this to any person." I continued to read the long message from my distraught mother, slowly finding myself getting more and more annoyed. Understand, this isn't the first time I received a message like this from my mom.

My mom would often send messages like this once she got fed up with me not communicating with her. While we were living together in the same house, I could quickly go 10 to 15 days without talking to her because we had gotten into such a big argument. After getting into one of our arguments, I would follow the same pattern: My blood boiled. I would be furious with my mom. Shame would wash over me for arguing. Then I would withdraw. That was the only way I knew how to cope with my emotions at the time, by simply not talking to her at all.

During this early adult life, I was 22-years-old, living at home for about six months. The previous four years before that, I lived without my mom at Georgetown in Washington, DC. After I graduated, I decided to move back to Weston, Florida, and live with my mom. Not because I wanted to, but because I had to. Quite frankly, in my first job out of school, as an IT recruiter, I wasn't making enough money to support myself, forcing me to live at home.

This was an awkward and embarrassing transition for me. While at Georgetown, I was used to having a high level of freedom. Living with my mom, in my mind, erased that freedom. She always wanted to know where I was going, who I would be with, and what time I would be home. These questions upset me immensely because I never had to tell her where I was going or when I was coming home when I was in school. Four years had gone by without me having to say anything to her about my whereabouts. So why was it that I must do it now? That was the story I continually told myself.

As a 22-year-old man, the fact that I was living with my mom crushed me. Deep down, I could only be mad at myself. In my mind, I was not a man because the life I envisioned living as a Georgetown graduate did not come to fruition. Thoughts of letting all the people around me down flooded my mind because I was living at home with my mom. I viewed myself as a failure because I didn't have a six-figure career. In hindsight, I foolishly thought as an 18-year-old entering college that my salary would be six figures when I graduated. This idea did not come with any real-life experience; instead, it was the story I made up in my head.

While living at home, whenever my mom asked me where I was going, I ignored her and kept her uninformed. In my opinion, I didn't have to tell her where I was going. There were zero reasons to let her know of my whereabouts and no need ever to check-in. If I did not tell her what I was doing, the way I looked at it somehow made me more man. If I was letting her keep tabs on me, that meant I was a boy. My misconstrued definition of manhood disabled me from effectively communicating with my mom. This still has me experience some moments of guilt today.

I've realized the anger that I displayed towards my mom had nothing to do with her. She was simply the scapegoat for my anger, frustration, and disappointment in myself. So much of my resentment towards myself stemmed from the narratives I created around how I was inadequate. I was mad at myself because I graduated from Georgetown and was still living at home. This caused me to feel like a failure because my postgraduate life was not starting the way it should. As far as I was concerned, all my peers were powerfully starting their lives. Foolishly, I compared my life to what I imagined all their lives looked like. Using comparison in this way was a fine form of self-sabotage. My self-sabotaging ways had me create a terrible relationship with myself. As a result of having such a terrible relationship with myself, it showed up like me making a terrible relationship with my mom.

I can see that my mom would always have the archetype of being a mother. No matter my age, she wanted to do everything in her power to take care of her son. That meant providing shelter, food, doing dishes for me, folding up my laundry, cleaning up my room, etc. All these things she wanted to do for me as a 22-year-old, was her way of showing love. Without a doubt, one of my mom's love languages was acts of service. It was apparent in how eager she was to do all these things for me. Yet, I could never truly appreciate all the helpful things she was doing for me because I had such a horrible relationship with myself and was so upset with how my life was going. So, whenever my mom cooked for me, I would get angry. Whenever my mom cleaned up after me, I would blow up and start an argument with her. Every time she washed, folded, and put away my clothes, I would yell at her. Every single time she asked me, "Where are you going? When will you be home? Who are you going out with?" I was ready to tell her off.

Back then, I truly believed we got into these arguments because she was infringing on my privacy, but truthfully, it's because I hated where I was in my life. It had nothing to do with my mom and everything to do with me. Living out those experiences taught me one of my biggest life lessons. What I realized is the most important relationship that I can have is my relationship with myself. My negative perception of my mom's actions was simply her trying to be the best mom that she could be. That entire time she was kind, helping me in whatever way she could and ultimately making sure I was safe. Instead of being grateful for that and appreciative of the amount of love she showed me, I would get furious. Not because of anything she was doing, but rather how I viewed what she was doing based on how I viewed myself.

Again, the apple does not fall far from the tree. My mom also had a terrible relationship with herself. Like I said before, all her validation was external validation. She wasn't healthy physically, emotionally, mentally, or spiritually. This resulted in her having low self-esteem, no confidence, and the inability to empower herself. She was rarely able to pick herself up. She lacked the tools to be kind, gentle, and graceful with herself consistently. What she thought would give her joy and love was doing things for me and everyone else. Through both my experiences and her experiences, I realize that the most important relationship I have is the relationship with myself. As a result, I take specific actions to consistently and intentionally improve my relationship with myself.

Developing daily practices over the last seven years has enabled me to view myself positively. One of the most impactful practices that I have implemented to date is gratitude journaling. Gratitude is a feeling of appreciation or thanks. By taking the time to pause, recognize the myriad of things I'm grateful for, acknowledge them, then appreciate them, always puts me in a state of peace and joy. During this process, I have learned to show gratitude for myself, what I've created, the courage I've shown, and the personal transformation I've made for the better.

My gratitude practice takes two different forms. The first is by thinking of one person or thing that I am grateful for. After choosing that specific person or something, I set a timer for ten minutes and write down all the reasons I am grateful for it. It astonishes me how deep into gratitude and appreciation I go as I freestyle write onto the pages of my journal. It creates a lightness in my body, a warm sensation in my heart, and a buzzing in my hands. I can feel the life force energy running deeply through my entire being by simply taking time to write down what I am grateful for and truly feel the gratitude within me.

The second form of gratitude focuses on being grateful for three things that I often take for granted. This includes being alive, having a roof over my head, having a comfortable bed, being able to afford high-quality food, my loving family and friends, a career I love, and so much more. It is so easy to focus on the things that I don't have. To combat this, I make a conscious effort to focus on what I do have. Knowing that I can create the life I desire is something I used to take for granted but is now a fixture in my heart. All because of gratitude.

In addition to gratitude journaling, I improve my relationship with myself by meditating, performing Tai Chi, sitting in ice baths, sweating in saunas, grounding my bare feet on lush grass, sleeping well, eating nutrient-dense foods, and moving my body. Performing all these activities from a place of love lets me build a greater relationship with myself because it fills my cup. Every time I eat nutrient-dense foods, the best quality meats I can find, and organic fruits and vegetables, these all provide me the fuel and energy I need to feel great. Making sure that I'm living in alignment with my values and principles, being my word, and practicing the Four Agreements by Don Miguel Ruiz all improve my relationship with myself. Thus, allowing me to have better relationships with my family, friends, and strangers.

Unfortunately, my mom wasn't taking the time to develop a great relationship with herself. While she was alive, I wasn't doing it either. I'm a firm believer that if she had a great relationship with herself, that maybe she wouldn't have gone out to get the cosmetic surgery that she was not healthy enough to get [and what led to her coma]. Perhaps she would not have sought outside interventions to improve the way she felt about herself.

Improving the relationship with self is one of the fundamental pillars of my work with clients. Helping them understand that doing their best to take care of themselves will put them in a better position to effectively relate to others, whether they are their loved ones, peers at work, or strangers.

The most effective way to have great relationships is by making sure we're doing things that take care of ourselves and improve our relationship first. My client, Elena, is a perfect embodiment of this. When Elena first came to me, she was disgusted with her body and disappointed with the relationships in her life. She desired to have a body she loved, a more intimate relationship with her partner, and closer relationships with her friends and family. From the outside looking in, Elena looked like she had it all. She excelled in her corporate career, owned a beautiful home, wore luxury fashion and accessories, and was always in the scene. She was the epitome of what being successful means by western standards: A great career, money, and influence. But deep down inside, she was miserable.

The first thing I asked her was to describe her relationship with herself. She was speechless. She didn't know what to say. She never thought about herself because she had been so externally focused on others for as long as she could remember. At work, all her actions were rooted in what she could do for her clients. How could she make their lives easier? How could she build those relationships stronger? At home, she was focused on what she could do to make her partner happy—thinking about how she could make his life more enjoyable. When it came to her friends, she would bend over backward to ensure their needs were being met. If one of her friends were going through a tough time, she would always lend a listening ear. If a friend were going through a breakup, she would be the one to take her out and help her forget about it. All the while, she had no systems or practices in place to improve her relationship with herself. She didn't even realize that was a thing.

I asked her very specific questions to uncover how she was treating herself. What are you doing for yourself to make you happy? What do you regularly do to make sure that you have the energy and vitality you need? Where do your needs fit in the pecking order in comparison to the many needs of your family, friends, partner, and clients? Very quickly, she realized that she was not intentionally doing anything for herself. There was not one current action that she was taking that she could honestly say she was doing for herself. Damn near everything was done for everyone else. She began to connect the dots and come to this conclusion herself.

The relationship with her partner, family, and friends wasn't where she wanted them to be because she didn't have a great relationship with herself. She realized that she was the common denominator in all those relationships. She concluded that the weight gain she experienced over the past three years resulted from her relationship with herself. She would emotionally eat when she felt upset with someone or stressed from work. Because she was exhausted after doing so much for others, she lacked the energy to move her body consistently. Not only did this negatively impact her physical body, but it hurt her emotionally, mentally, and spiritually as well. She was constantly sad, anxious, angry, and unfulfilled.

Now she was aware that all these stressors caused her poor relationship with herself, negatively impacting her relationships. It all made sense to her now. She could see how she was resentful towards her friends because she felt like she was giving so much to them but not getting the same level of friendship in return. She could now see why she thought her family did not honestly give her the love she desired. She could see why she had such a short temper with her partner. Slowly but surely, she realized it was not those people who were to blame; it was the absence of care for herself that had her feel this way.

With this new level of clarity, she committed to improving her relationship with herself. She started developing her values, connection, and career values because she saw that her improvements began with herself. She used those values as a filter to make better decisions for herself. These decisions started with making intentional time for herself. We co-created a morning routine where she wrote down one thing she was grateful for, got 30 minutes of movement in, and ate a nutrient-dense breakfast. This had her start her day feeling great physically, emotionally, mentally, and spiritually.

She found that taking care of herself was not selfish but necessary. She was smiling more. She was laughing more. She had gratitude for herself and those around her. Self-care and deepening the relationship with self became a catalyst for improving her relationships. Over weeks, the relationships that mattered most in her life improved. She now has a thriving relationship with her partner, a close connection to her family, friendships she cherishes, and work relationships that energize her. All of which was possible because of her commitment to improving her relationship with herself.

 What You Can Stop Doing

Stop neglecting your relationship with yourself. Stop thinking that taking care of yourself first is selfish.

 What You Can Start Doing

Consciously and intentionally develop a better relationship with yourself. Understand that taking care of yourself puts you in a position to have a great relationship with yourself and others.

 How You Can 2

Get clear on what your values are. Once you are clear on these values, embody them, and practice living them out every day. Perform gratitude journaling every morning by bringing awareness to your appreciation for all you create in your life. Recognize yourself for all the amazing work you are doing for yourself and those around you.

Chapter 5: Unsolicited Help

"You can't help someone who does
not want to help themselves."
- Unknown

The date is June 2013. One of my best friends, Adam, asked me if I could design a TRX workout program for him to perform at home. I was about a year deep in being a personal trainer and a sports performance coach at this point in my career. Adam was training with me for the last few months to improve his strength, conditioning, and physique. He put a small team together to take his physical health to the next level. Mark, one of his closest friends, who was well-versed in diet and nutrition, was there to give him his meal plan. My purpose was to provide him with an in-home training program to complement his work with me in the gym. The overall intention was for the three of us to collaborate on the sole goal of helping Adam take his physical body and health to the next level.

I was two years removed from my football career and focused on getting in the best physical shape of my life. My days consisted of hitting my training hard, absorbing as much new information as possible, bettering myself, and helping others do the same. I felt extremely confident in my abilities to put a great program together for Adam. In addition to physical fitness, I thought I knew a significant amount about nutrition as well. However, Mark's conversation with Adam completely changed my view on food and, ultimately, my life.

As Mark, Adam, and I were all sitting together, Mark shared the nutrition program that Adam would follow. Mark wanted Adam to start eating grass-fed red meat, pasture-raised eggs with the yolk included (crazy, I know!), organic fruits and vegetables, and a variety of animal fats in his diet, such as raw dairy and grass-fed butter, all while cutting out all the processed foods and vegetable oils.

I was shocked! The diet that Mark was describing vastly differed from the type of diet I was following at the time. My diet was more of what I now call a "politically correct" diet. This diet consisted of lean protein sources like chicken breast, tilapia, lean cuts of beef (occasionally), and all the protein powder I could get my hands on. For carbohydrates, I was eating slow-burning, complex carbs like brown rice and sweet potatoes. Fruit and vegetables were part of my diet as well. Any form of dairy was an absolute no-no. There was no emphasis on the quality of this food and whether it was organic or not.

As I was intently and somewhat skeptically listening to Mark explain to Adam all these foods that he was going to eat, I was consciously thinking about how there was no way this nutrition plan would work. I could not fathom melting grass-fed butter on vegetables, using organic and raw heavy cream to make shakes and smoothies, or eating a ton of grass-fed beef throughout the week could provide optimal health? I remember thinking to myself, "Mark is crazy!"

In my head, Mark didn't know what he was talking about. Selfishly, I believed that Mark was going to sabotage Adam's results. Consequently, that was going to make me look bad as his trainer. I was thinking, "Mark is going to mess up my credibility as a great trainer and no one is going to want to work with me. I won't let this happen!" All I could think about was how the amazing training program that I put together would be viewed as trash! This would all be Mark's fault. After what seemed like hours went by, Adam left the room for a moment. Now it was just Mark and me at the table. This whole time, in my head, I was questioning his knowledge and ability to build an effective nutrition program for our friend.

Mark was very accomplished up to this point in his life. He was 25-years-old and had been a high-level athlete his entire life. He studied at the University of Florida and was extremely knowledgeable about nutrition, movement, and how to build a vibrant body overall. One that could handle the stresses of everyday life and not only address those stresses but also thrive in any environment. Looking back, I can see that Mark was way ahead of his time! But my ego didn't quite allow me to believe him at that moment.

Once Adam walked away, Mark and I were sitting at the table when I hurried up close to him and whispered, "You're telling me that Adam is going to eat all of those foods and lose weight?" Mark confidently replied, "Of course." Curiously I asked him, "So let me get this straight… you're telling me that if I wanted to do this same type of diet to lose weight, I would do the same thing, but I would just eat smaller quantities?" He passionately explained, "No, no, no, you would eat more food because you're much bigger than he is." In astonishment, I blurted, "Get the fuck out!" I did not believe him.

Based on my knowledge, my whole idea of losing weight was strictly calories in versus calories out. It had nothing to do with the actual foods themselves. Mark and I were having dialogue back and forth, where now I was the person being consulted. Mark said, "Look, Danny, I will send you some information that you can look into. Dive into this information, do your research, and come to your conclusions.

If this sounds like something that you think can help you, I'll be glad to write you a nutrition program. Nodding my head up and down, I say, "Okay, perfect."

To a certain extent, I was open-minded when it came to learning new information that could provide new tools, tactics, and strategies that would allow me to hit my weight goal. Looking into different research was fun for me, and I enjoyed coming up with my conclusions. This fit right up my alley. That night, I went home, and the first resource I looked at was the work of Dr. Weston A. Price.

Dr. Price was a dentist in Cleveland during the early 1900s. He saw that all his patients who had tooth decay, cavities, or some physical degeneration in their jaw structure had terrible overall physical health. This led him to wonder what the connection was between what a person is eating, their oral health, and their physical health overall. This led him to redirect his work towards nutrition. He went on many expeditions across the world, researching civilizations that were still eating their traditional foods. Because these were isolated populations, no industrial food or industrial agriculture had made it to those places. That meant no canned foods, processed foods, or vegetable oils in any of these cultures' diets.

He found that all these people, whether African, European, from the Mediterranean, or Asian populations, ate their traditional diet, meaning they ate the foods grown in abundance in their area. They also ate many animal lumps of meat and animal products based on their access to animals. What fascinated me most was how he noticed that all these people had amazing teeth, symmetrical facial structures, and great overall health.

Most of these populations didn't have a word for heart disease or comment for cancer because it didn't exist. Out of all the people he researched, we're talking thousands of mouths; he would find one cavity for every one hundred mouths he tested. Whereas back home in Ohio, most of his patients had multiple cavities. What he saw was that these indigenous people had perfectly straight teeth, no crowding of the teeth, and while their teeth were slimy because they didn't brush them, they all had strong oral health and great health overall. The connection that he put together was how important it was to eat high-quality animal foods and stay away from all processed foods simultaneously. These people had terrific, robust health because their diets were rich in fat-soluble vitamins and enzymes. Processed foods, on the other hand, were devoid of this.

When you fast forward during Weston A. Price's longitudinal studies, he found that these same people in the next generation had vastly different health outcomes. This occurred once roads started to reach their communities, and they began to be introduced to Western food, such as white sugar, white flour, and vegetable oils. They started to see that the next generation of kids was born with a smaller cranial structure. Their jawlines were much smaller, so all their teeth didn't fit properly in their mouths, causing crowding. Their face didn't grow in equal thirds, where the top third of their forehead to the top of their nose was not equal to the top of the nose to the top of the lip and not equal from the top of the lip to the bottom of the jaw.

These kids were not physically healthy because they started eating many processed foods and started getting away from their traditional diet. Later in the studies, it showed that they were able to reverse this with the next generation of kids if both parents started eating the nutrient-dense, quality foods that were high in vitamin A, vitamin D, and vitamin K, all of which were prevalent in high-quality animal products, especially the organ meats.

Upon meticulously reviewing all this research, I was floored. I could not believe that a person could have great health by eating things like grass-fed red meat, butter, raw dairy, organs, and of course, eating a variety of organic vegetables, some fruits, grains, and tubers that were natural to their culture. By reading all of this, I found out that everything I learned about nutrition up to that point wasn't serving me. Eating a low-fat diet was not helping me. Eating lean protein sources that were coming from sick animals was making me sick. Once I saw all this information, I invested a few hundred dollars and started working with Mark. Mark printed out an entire meal plan that allowed me to go to the grocery store and learn how to pick out the foods that would work best for me. To maximize my results, I decided to go all-in and quit drinking alcohol as well.

At that time of my life as a young 24-year-old, I formed some destructive habits. Before becoming a personal trainer and sports performance coach, I worked corporate jobs that I hated. During my corporate career, I impatiently waited to get to Friday night, so I could hit happy hour, party for the night, and drink throughout the entire weekend. I was drinking my problems and insecurities away in the process. Sunday would come, and I would already be lamenting that Monday was right around the corner. Even when I transitioned into the fitness industry, I still partied hard on the weekends, drank a ton, ate at Denny's at 4 AM, and ultimately woke up on Saturday and did the same thing again. Now that I was getting ready to embark on this new food journey, I decided to cut out drinking altogether, stop smoking weed for the time being, and cut out any processed foods.

At that time, I had already lost about fifteen pounds from playing football, dropping down from about 285 pounds and was sitting somewhere between 265 to 270 pounds. Once I changed the way I ate, I ended up dropping another 35 pounds in about five months. The weight was melting off me. The only thing that I changed was my nutrition. I was eating whole nutrient-dense foods and completely cut out all the processed food. That included canned foods, low-quality deli meats, chips, crackers, cereals, microwave dinners, cakes, etc. I wasn't drinking any alcohol, juice, or sugary sports drinks at that time. Initially, my goal with losing weight was to be leaner. In my mind, if I lost a bunch of weight, I would get a bunch of girls. The formula was simple: Less weight = more women. Even though that was never a problem at the time, it shows where my mindset was.

After a few months, I couldn't believe the results I had achieved. Not only did I lose the weight, which was amazing, but it was like a veil was lifted over my head. My mood and personality completely shifted: less irritable, less angry, more joyful. My energy completely leveled up. Naps were no longer a part of my daily routine. Instead of getting sick and having colds a couple of times a year, I found that I was never getting sick. I was vibrant, vital, and healthy. This lifestyle change worked for me in ways I never imagined.

My success had me realize, "Wow! My mom could do all these same things and she would get amazing results!" I thought to myself, "Maybe she will lose more weight. Maybe she will gain more energy. She can create more confidence in herself. She'll be able to stop taking many of her medications because she won't be in as much pain. She won't need her opioid medication." This was reminiscent of how I felt when I saw how alive my mom looked when Coach Kelly visited my house during my senior year of high school. I was committed to helping my mom transform her health and life!

It's funny; I can vividly remember trying to get my mom to make these changes after I'd been implementing them for about six months. She didn't have it. She didn't want to do it. But I wasn't taking no for an answer. I said to myself, "I'm going to make this change happen. I'm going to help her create a healthy life!" This was not effective AT ALL! One day, my mom came home with about $200 worth of groceries. Upon examining the groceries, I immediately told her everything she needed to get rid of. "No, we can't have this. It's not cooked in the right oil. No, we can't have this, it's processed. No, why did you get that chicken? It's not pasture-raised. Why did you get that type of beef? it's not grass fed. No, that fish isn't wild-caught, that's not good enough." This whole time, I'm telling my mom how everything she was doing was not good enough. She needed to change all of it. She needed to do it my way. I realize how annoying this is.

Frankly, my mom told me, "I don't want to change this. I like how I'm doing it. This is working for me." Perspective is such a funny thing. She perceived that her style of eating was working for her. I perceived that she wasn't doing the right things. We were both coming from our perspectives, being righteous in the process. My mom was in pain for much of my life. Based on how much less pain I was physically, mentally and emotionally because I changed my food, I wanted my mom to do the same thing. In my heart, I was coming from a place of love. Changing my mom's health meant the world to me, even if that meant forcing her to try to do it. If I had to nag her about her food choices every day, I was committed to doing it! As time went on, I continued to make slick comments about her way being ineffective. My mom still didn't change.

When she wouldn't change or listen to me, I took it personally. This caused me to be upset with her, which led to fights, arguments, disagreements, and me not talking to her for days at a time. Again, this is all because of where I was in my life. This was me trying to change her when she wasn't ready to change herself. During this unproductive process, I would lose my peace. When she wasn't doing all the things that I felt she was supposed to do, I would fall back into the ways of being that no longer served me: anger, frustration, forcefulness. All of which would show up in how I acted towards her.

I learned from this experience with my mom that I couldn't help someone change until they're ready to change themselves. Trying to get my mom to change based on the changes I made was highly unsuccessful. My error in thinking was the belief that she was going to change because I changed. However, I was ready and committed to making those changes, while she was not. To me, it was worth spending the extra money to buy the highest quality food. Tapping into discipline excited me. This was the first time I experienced accurate alignment in my goals and actions. That's what prevented me from going to Taco Bell, Wendy's, ordering pizza, and eating at Denny's late at night. These were all habits I developed for years, forming food addictions in the process. But the difference was my readiness to change.

What I didn't realize at the time was that I couldn't force my mom to change. I could only be there for her when she was ready to change and would like my help in that process. At the time, I didn't know that. Now I realize in my life that I can only help someone change when they're ready. That's what I focus on now in my work with all my clients. They come to me when they're prepared to change. I don't approach them and say, "Hey, I see you are self-sabotaging in this way. Come work with me. I see all the ineffective habits that you have. You should come work with me." No, it doesn't work that way. It only works when that person is ready to make the change and wants my help.

This reminds me of my client, Eugene. Eugene was very much like me. He has gone through the process of bettering his health by eating better, actively managing his stress, and filling his cup in a way that allows him to experience joy and fulfillment in his life. However, he sees his mom is not putting in that type of work. He and his mom would get into arguments stemming from his mom's lack of desire to work on herself. One day he came to me and said, "Hey, what can I do to help my mom change? I don't want to have these types of arguments anymore. I no longer desire to be on the receiving end of all the nasty things she says because she doesn't feel good."

I said, "Eugene, I 100% understand where you're coming from. What you're saying hits home so deeply because I know what it's like to want to change your mom." Compassionately, I explained, "You can't change your mom until your mom is ready to change herself." This wasn't what Eugene wanted to hear. It took time to resonate. He started to realize that his wanting to change his mom, expending his energy, banging his head against a brick wall to get her to change was not working. He realized he was losing his peace and that he was taking away from himself. His energy waned. Over time he was able to recognize that that was no longer serving him.

Since then, he's been doing his best to lead by example, continuing to meditate, do his Tai Chi, go on his walks, consistently exercise, and eat well. Now his mom joins him on some of those walks. His mom has meditated with him a few times. His mom will enjoy a better meal with him a few times throughout the week. That brings Eugene much more peace and happiness because he realizes that he can only change himself and be there for his mom when she's ready to change. When she is ready to go all-in with her lifestyle changes, he will support her. He's seen the glimpses. He's seen what's possible. Most of all, his peace is protected because he's focusing solely on the things he can control, leading by example, and ready to help when his mom is ready.

 What You Can Stop Doing

Stop trying to change someone that isn't ready to change himself.

 What You Can Start Doing

Be patient and unattached. When the person is ready to change, he will reach out to you.

 How You Can 2

Lead by example. Let the way you live your life be an inspiration and proof of what is possible. Solely focus on what you can control: your words and actions.

Chapter 6. Here When You're Ready

*"You have to meet people where they are, and
sometimes you have to leave them there."*
- Iyanla Vanzant

Towards the end of 2014, my mom started making some incredible changes for herself. Every morning, she would wake up, go to our small neighborhood pool and swim laps for two to three hours throughout the day. This was a massive shift from who my mom was in all the years before; she was the person who would spend every single day in the house and on her bed.

I can vividly remember getting myself up to get ready for school in my early high school years. Since school started just after 7 AM, I would leave the house around 6:30 AM, and my mom would still be asleep. This made perfect sense. It was early in the morning; my mom did not work, so she had no reason to be up at that time. I would perform my regular high school daily routine: Drive to school, attend football practice for two hours, hang out with some friends afterward, and return home around 8 PM. When I walked back inside my house, I would see my mom fast asleep in her bed. Logically, it was because she had a long day doing whatever it was that kept her busy. Once 8 PM rolled around, I assumed she went to bed early after having a long day.

It wasn't until I was an adult that I realized my mom was knocked out from her prescription drugs most of those times. The opioid medication that she took had her passed out for hours upon hours on end. Often, she would only leave that bed to use the bathroom and maybe eat some food. Fast forward about nine years later, and I would see my mom waking up diligently every morning to get her laps in at the pool. She was exercising, getting fresh air, getting sunlight. It was amazing.

Not only would my mom get her swimming in, but she would also walk around the neighborhood with her walker. She had this little red walker that she was always clinging to outside with her oversized floral shirt, baggy pants, white Sketchers, and matching white headband. Initially, she would walk for only two or three minutes at a time. That all her body was capable of at the time. Slowly, it built up to 20 minutes, 30 minutes, until she was pushing towards an hour, consistently walking around the neighborhood.

Again, this is the same person who, just nine years earlier, when I was in high school, would travel around our small two-bedroom home with her wheelchair. She would use the wheelchair to move as little as 30 feet from her bed to the bathroom or kitchen. She would park the wheelchair outside the bathroom door, go into the bathroom, use the bathroom, come back out, sit back inside of the wheelchair, then scoot herself about six, seven feet to the kitchen, and roam around the kitchen while sitting in her wheelchair. Then she would take the wheelchair back another 30 feet to get back into her bed.

She would traverse that little triangle for years upon years, never actually thinking that she could fully walk around the house without that wheelchair. Witnessing the transformation of her mobility and activity was inspiring. She even started to eat whole foods: chicken, beef, turkey, fish, fruits, vegetables, potatoes, rice. She would buy all-natural food from the grocery store instead of TV dinners, Lean

Cuisines, Smart Choices, and Weight Watchers meals. My mom lived on these microwave dinners, and so did I. As I was eating much better, she eventually started making huge changes by eating real food independently. It was unbelievable.

As my mom became more active and ate better, it inspired her to be more social. She had a guy she was seeing that used to be an old fling or a boyfriend of sorts, located near where she grew up in New Jersey. She would travel and see him from time to time, and he would come down to South Florida to visit her. Before that, my mom was never getting on planes or traveling to see friends and family. Now she was meeting friends out and about for lunches instead of only having conversations on the phone. She was making tremendous changes in her life. However, for me during that time, it wasn't enough.

I spent more than two years as a sports performance coach, personal trainer, and nutrition coach. My knowledge base was growing, I was improving my health by leaps and bounds, and I was helping my clients do the same. While my mom was making incredible strides, I thought she could still be doing more. From my point of view, it wasn't enough that she was going outside, swimming, walking to the best of her abilities, and eating real food. What I desired more than anything was for my mom to be doing these things the EXACT way that I wanted them to be done.

When it came to her food, it wasn't good enough that she was eating chicken. It had to be pasture-raised chicken. It wasn't good enough that she was eating beef. It had to be 100% grass-fed, grass-finished beef. It wasn't good enough that she was eating fish. It needed to be wild-caught fish. It wasn't good enough that she was eating fruits and vegetables. She needed to be eating organic fruits and vegetables.

Those were my criticisms at that time. Nothing that she was doing was good enough for me. Her amazing effort, the turnaround she made in her lifestyle were insufficient. She wasn't following the workout plan that I thought she should be doing. She wasn't doing the amount of strenuous activity that I thought she should be doing. As I reflect on it, I can see how wrong I was. My lapse in judgment was thinking that my mom needed to do everything my way. My problem was that I never met my mom where she was at. Instead of being proud of, inspired by, and supportive of all the incremental, positive changes my mom made, I strictly saw it as my mom not doing enough. Instead of having my mom's back, encouraging her, and being her biggest cheerleader, I pointed out everything I perceived she was doing wrong. The small amount of praise that I gave her would be overshadowed by larger amounts of criticism. I would say to my mom, "Your meal can be better by doing this." "Wow! I love that you're walking. But now you need to do more."

In hindsight, I can see that I was never meeting my mom where she was at. By this, I mean putting aside my desires for my mom, whether those desires were in service for her or not, and endeavouring to understand where she was in her journey. I should have asked myself, "How can I be in support of her and help her based on what she is ready, willing, and committed to doing?" It wasn't about me. It should never have been about me. Yet, I made it about me the whole time. As a result, I selfishly didn't believe my mom was doing enough to improve her life.

This negatively impacted the way I showed up for her, preventing me from giving her words of affirmation or letting her know how much I appreciated the changes she did make. My mom greatly appreciated acts of service. There were plenty of actions I could have taken to show her how much I cared about the improvements she made. Worst of all, I was withholding love from her because I didn't feel like she was doing enough. So much of how I punished my mom was through withholding my love from her. Whether that was by not speaking to her, whether by not spending time with her, or not keeping her informed on what was going on in my life, I punished my mom because I was upset that she wasn't doing "enough." In my mind, her not making her health and lifestyle changes in my exact vision of what it was supposed to look like had me act in ways I still regret today.

It took an immense amount of soul searching to realize that how I treated her had nothing to do with her and everything to do with me. She was doing the best she could with the information she had. Yet, from my standpoint and my limiting beliefs, I realized that so much of the love I had for my mom in the last few years of her life was conditional. There was little unconditional love on my part. It was more "if you eat this organic food, these grass-fed, pastured meats, then I'm going to love you." "When you exercise for this amount of time and do these types of workouts, then I'm going to love you." "When you are doing the things that I expect you to be doing, then I'm going to love you." This crushed my mom.

It hurts to realize just how shitty of a person I was to her. This was the most important person in my life, who always loved me unconditionally and would do anything to succeed, be happy, and be fulfilled. This heart-breaking lesson has been one of the foundational lessons that I have learned in my life: To meet people where they are.

Meeting someone where they are at is one of my most painful life lessons. Holding myself accountable for how I was with my mom in the last year of her life is one of the hardest things I've had to forgive myself for. No matter who the person is, whether it's someone I'm working with, a family member, or a stranger, I get to meet that person where they're at. What that means to me is that wherever that person is, whatever that person is ready to do to create a change, that's the place we're going to start. If a client of mine is committed to making one change in the next three months, then that's the one thing we're going to focus on.

It's not on me to tell my client that they need to add another 10 to 15 things to their list. No, it's not about me. It's about the client. Every time I work closely with someone, I make it a point to deeply understand that person, their goals, and where they aspire to be. Most importantly, we get to be clear on where they currently are to start from that place and move forward from there.

It is of the utmost importance for me to meet my clients where they are, but they must do the same. I've had countless experiences with men and women who were so fed up with where they were in life, how they let themselves go, how they lost their sense of self, that they would beat themselves up for it. By beating themselves up, they created a vicious cycle where they would get depressed thinking about how their life or body used to look, have negative thoughts and beliefs about who they currently are, and take action that reinforced their thoughts. This would lead to more depression, more negative thoughts and beliefs, and more self-sabotaging actions.

For example, a woman gets depressed when she realizes none of her clothes fit like they used to. She thinks about how undisciplined she is, compares herself to her friend that lost her baby weight fast, and next thing she knows, she is in a McDonald's drive-through ordering a McFlurry only to wake up the next day feeling guilty and more depressed.

Reframing their mindset around how they view themselves is the first step for my clients to create their dream life. Instead of beating themselves up about how they got to where they are, we acknowledge that this is the current place they are at. It does not mean that they must be in love with where they currently are, but they get to let go of all the thoughts, words, and actions that got them there. These thoughts, words, and actions that got them into this state will not get them out of it. Once we establish this principle, the client can move forward proactively.

I have a client, Stephanie, who is an amazing woman. During her intake process, she noticed so many aspects of her life that she wanted to improve. She wanted to improve her physical health. She was overweight, weak, had low energy, and a low sex drive. She wished to improve her mental and emotional health. Throughout the previous three years of her life, she constantly found herself on edge, anxious, angry, and ready to erupt when someone said the wrong thing at the wrong time. She wanted to improve her relationship with her son and be the best mother possible. She felt that she was not spending enough time with him because of her decreased vitality and high-stress levels. She wanted to be a great leader to all her employees. She shared with me how she could tell that the people she managed were afraid to be honest with her, fearing being yelled at and scrutinized by her. This resulted in her not getting the proper feedback she needed to improve projects for clients and stagnation of her company's growth.

She knew this was a problem and that something needed to change. Her life was not working for her at that time. Overall, she realized that so many domains of her life could use huge improvements and she was committed to making it happen. She wanted to work on all aspects of her life simultaneously, thinking this would create the biggest changes in the fastest way possible. We sat down, created clarity, and developed a game plan where we both committed to meeting her where she was.

We agreed to pick three distinct changes to focus on first. Those three things came from her as opposed to me telling her that she had to start with those three things. No. It was her empowering herself by deciding how she was going to start. My role was to help her brainstorm which things she would begin with and realistically apply them to her life. The three things that we started with were eliminating the processed foods from her diet, practicing gratitude journaling every day, and spending quality time with her son. By focusing on those three goals and doing them to the highest of her capabilities, she transformed how she showed up in her life, which positively impacted how she showed up in the people around her.

As she mastered those three goals, she could feel the impact these improvements made on her life. They became a catalyst for her to continue to make new goals, accomplish them, and grow. Now she's at a point where she is constantly leveling up. Month after month, she's achieving new feats. She feels so much fulfillment because she's now confident in her ability to achieve what she sets out to do—grounding herself in the idea that she can move forward with new goals by first meeting where she is.

A massive reason for this success was because she got unequivocal on the specific actions she was willing to take. I met her right there. From that place, she accomplished those goals, celebrated herself, felt a sense of joy and fulfillment, and used that energy to go forward, make new goals, and achieve those goals in her life. Now she sees that she's capable of anything that she puts her time, energy, and focus into—

making sure that she first meets herself where she is in the process.

 ### What You Can Stop Doing

Stop letting your expectations of where you think you or someone else "should be" cause you to treat yourself or others like crap.

 ### What You Can Start Doing

Meet yourself where you are at. Meet others where they are at.

 ### How You Can 2

As it pertains to yourself, get clear on where you currently are (not where you think you should be). From this clear understanding, decide where you desire to go or what you would like to achieve. Create a realistic plan that will allow you to fill this gap.

As it pertains to others, communicate with them how you can be of service. Don't be attached to your way of doing things. Find out what the other person is willing to do and help them move forward from that place. Co-create and collaborate.

Chapter 7: Boundaries Create Clarity

"When we fail to set boundaries and hold people accountable, we feel used and mistreated."
- Brene Brown

It was a beautiful fall day on the hilltop at Georgetown University in Washington, DC. My first few months on campus brought me immense joy. Being a student-athlete, playing football, the sport I love, creating new relationships, and forming deep friendships excited me. I was learning and having so much fun living independently, making sense of myself, and becoming my own man. Suddenly, I felt my phone vibrate. I reached into my pocket, pulled out my Sidekick LX cell phone, looked at it, and saw that my mom was calling me again. It's Friday, the fifth day of the week, the fifth time that my mom has called me this week. Somewhat annoyed, I picked up the phone, "Hey, mom, how are you doing?" She replies, "I'm good. How is your day going?

We essentially went through the same small talk that we had the previous four days. She inquired, "How are you enjoying the class? How's football going? Are you making any new friends?" This when I remember my conversations starting to get very short with my mom. There was resentment building within me because she kept calling me over and over again. It was overwhelming. It was too much. These are my first three months being out on my own and living away from home. Yet, I felt like I was still at home because of how often my mom would call me. This had me feeling like a little boy. I thought I was caged in.

I created a story in my head that if I consistently spoke to my mom every single day, sometimes multiple times in one day, it would stunt my growth. In my head, no one else's parents were doing this. Everyone else had the freedom to learn about themselves, go about their life, and essentially live as a free young human being. During our many calls after that one, my frustration started to show. My answers started to get extremely short with my mom. Every time she called, I would annoyingly ask, "What do you want, mom?" "Yes, mom, I'm good." Hey mom, I need to go. Okay, mom. Love you. Bye."

At the time, I never realized how much this truly crumpled my mom's heart. This had her feel sad, unwanted, and unappreciated, all things that she would continue to echo later in our relationship. One night during the first semester of my freshman year, I had a tough conversation with my mom, where I let her know that she could not call me every day anymore. I voiced my frustration to her, telling her how embarrassed I was each time she called me when I was out with friends. I explained to her that for me to grow and be the man that I wanted to be, I couldn't have her calling me every day, or multiple times a day, as I was out and about trying to create this new life of mine. This is the first time I remember creating a boundary with my mom. However, the way I made this boundary wasn't healthy. It came from a place of anger. It was generated out of frustration. Ultimately, me creating this boundary was me telling my mom to leave me the hell alone.

This would continue to play out once I moved back home after graduating from Georgetown. Not only would I lack boundaries with my mom, but she would also have a lack of boundaries with me. This showed up in a relationship that my mom started to develop in the final years of her life.

She was dating this guy a few years after I had moved back in with her (the same guy from chapter six). This man was from a previous relationship she had when she was in high school in New Jersey. Through Facebook, they got back in touch and started building a friendship. Over time, this friendship started to build into much more, at least in my mom's mind. Before I knew it, every single day, she was having a conversation with this guy named Steve. Right away, I knew I didn't like it. Steve lived back in New Jersey while my mom was down in Weston, Florida. She constantly had conversations with him. Part of me was happy that my mom was having conversations with a friend and being more social. That was until a specific day occurred that I will never forget.

It was a dark, gloomy, rainy day in October of 2013. I had just gotten back home from work and I found my mom crying in her bed. Deeply concerned, I asked my mom, "What's wrong? What happened?" She began to tell me about her relationship with Steve. Something that we never deeply explored together. Quite frankly, I never really cared to ask her about it. As she attempted to wipe her tears and catch her breath, she told me that Steve called her and said she's no longer allowed to call him but that only he can call her. He continued on to say he recently changed his number so that she could not contact him.

When my mom told me this, I thought it was strange and was immediately on defense. I inquired, "Why is it that only he can call you, and you can't call him?" She began to go deeper into the story telling me how Steve and his wife…Yes, his wife, had been separated for some time now but still lived together. Since they lived together, Steve didn't want his wife to get the wrong idea about my mom calling him. I went from feeling a bit defensive to flat-out furious. I could tell when someone was getting played, and my mom was getting played. She didn't see it like that, though. "No, no, no, they're going through a separation. They're not together. They just continued to live together for money reasons, and it makes it easier." My mom assured me. Bullshit. My mom was making excuses for this guy, the same guy that had been showing her a lot of attention. My mom was blinded because she was missing that type of attention from a man for a long time.

My mom had been single for pretty much my entire life. My dad was in and out of the picture. My mom kicked him out when I was three, then he moved back in when I was in 5th grade, then got kicked out again when I was in 7th grade. Safe to say, it wasn't the healthiest relationship. She never had a man in her life that truly appreciated her and deeply loved her. To my mom, Steve was this person. Steve was the person who would sit there and have deep, long conversations with her. Steve was the guy that would say all the things that my mom wanted to hear. It was clear to me how much my mom liked Steve. Evidenced by the big smile on her face, belly laughter, and vitality she showed when on the phone with him.

I was fine with her talking with Steve, but after learning he was still married, living with his wife, and then told my mom she could not call him, I never looked at Steve the same way again. Every time I came home and found my mom talking to Steve, I would get pissed. When she was off the phone, I would look at her and judgingly say, "What the hell are you doing? This guy's playing you. Do you think it makes sense that you're not allowed to call him, but he's allowed to call you? You don't even have his phone number. He calls from a blocked number every time so that you don't have his number and so that you can't call him directly!"

This irritated me so much. So, what did I do? I lectured my mom every single day. I would always tell her, "Stop talking to him! Why are you allowing yourself to get played? You're playing yourself. Stop talking to him!" If you've ever had a friend getting played by someone they are in love with, you know how ineffective lecturing is. She would never listen.

What I recognized is that this was an opportunity for my mom to create a boundary with me. Yes, I was concerned for her as her son, but she was a grown-ass woman. Whoever she was deciding to have a relationship with was entirely up to her. It had nothing to do with me. Yet, it was almost like I was trying to flip the script, attempting to be her parent in that situation. My priority was to prevent him from being hurt, having and heartbroken, and being let down. Yet, I now realize that that wasn't my place. It wasn't my business at all. Yes, that's my mom, and I love my mom dearly. But she gets to decide how she wants to spend her time and who she spent it with. She would travel up to New Jersey to see Steve. Every time she came back from one of those weekends, her whole mood was different, she came back excited, energetic, and joyful.

Instead of being happy for her in these moments, I was mad and fearful that she would get hurt. The truth of the matter is that she was having a good time. She was fine with what was going on and what their dynamic was. Did I agree with it? No. But I could have decided to be happy for her, or at the very least, recognize it was not my place to meddle. My mom and Steve ended up having this relationship up until the day that she passed away.

Having healthy boundaries with people is so important. When my mom was calling me in college and trying to do things for me when I lived with her after college, I realized that she was doing these things out of love. Yet, I was bothered by it so much because I felt like it was impeding upon the boundaries that I had created in my head. The problem is, I did not communicate these boundaries with my mom, they only excited it in my world. My mom didn't even know they existed. They were not clear at all. Only in communicating them to her, could she know they exist, and we could better understand what was acceptable and what wasn't in our relationship. Most of us walk around with expectations in our head that we never communicate, then have the audacity to get mad when people don't read our minds.

My mom could have also placed boundaries on her relationship with Steve. If she had created boundaries around what I was allowed to ask her or what I was allowed to say regarding their relationship, maybe there would have been fewer arguments around whether she should be with him or not. Since those boundaries were not in place, I thought I could express whatever I wanted to say to her about their relationship. I allowed myself to think that I could share my point of view even when it wasn't welcomed.

I realize how important it is to have healthy boundaries with all the people in my life, whether personally, relationally, or professionally. These boundaries are created based on my values, principles, and ultimately how I want to live my life. This enables me to give other people I have relationships with a clear set of guidelines that they can follow for our relationship and our interactions. I invite them to do the same thing with me and create boundaries around how they want my relationship with them to look as well. Setting boundaries doesn't mean there will not be any conflict, but it lowers the chance that you will get upset because someone crossed an imaginary line they didn't know existed.

Boundaries are like the rules in sports. They create the guidelines so that we know how to play with each other, interact with each other, and understand what's acceptable and not acceptable. This way, it's possible to have loving, respectful relationships with our friends, family, loved ones, colleagues, and even strangers. Boundaries are the ultimate way that we can show respect to other people. This is something that I think is critical for all relationships.

Boundaries are foundational in my work with clients. A lack of boundaries is a common reason why people have resentment towards others. As a result, my clients and I make it a point to work on this at the very beginning of our programs together. This creates the rules and sets the guidelines of how we will work together, how they will live their lives, and how they will interact with those people in their lives.

This reminds me of one of my clients, Jack. For a long time, Jack was the go-to person for his mom to vent about every problem she was going through. This started when Jack was just a little boy, around five old. Whenever there was a problem or mom was upset, she would seek out Jack. Jack allowed this to happen for about 18 years. He didn't realize how draining this was to him. He didn't know how sad he would get every time his mom came and dropped all her baggage on him. At first, he enjoyed doing it because he saw how much better it made his mom feel. After unloading all her stress, sadness, and frustrations, it seemed like 100 pounds of stress were lifted from her shoulders. Jack liked that his mom felt better, but he didn't realize how shitty it made him think for all these years.

In our third session together, we dove deep to unpack this. He built awareness that he felt drained, depleted, sad, anxious, and depressed after his mom dumped all her baggage onto him. The 100 pounds would transfer from her shoulders to his. He could recall dozens of times in his life when his energy and mood would shift from a high state to a low one after his mom had one of these venting sessions with him. Now he was piecing together how this shift in his energy and mood negatively impacted his interactions with his girlfriend, friends, co-workers, and strangers. This new level of awareness inspired him to make new choices with his mom going forward.

He realized that there were boundaries that got to be set between him and his mom. While he felt very uncomfortable about how his mom would react to his requests, he knew it was something that he needed to do for himself. He courageously decided to act. He made a delicious dinner for him and his mom. Dinner was when they typically sat down together each day and was often the time his mom wanted to vent to him.

He started the conversation by telling his mom how much he loves and appreciates her. He expressed how there was no way he would be where he is in his life if it wasn't for her. From there, he shared how he felt when his mom would vent to him, explaining the feelings of sadness, frustration, anxiousness, and depression he would experience during these times. There and then, he requested that she would no longer drop the heavy, negative baggage on him. He explained that they're allowed to have conversations, interact with each other, love each other, and hold space for each other.

His mom had no idea how much her venting negatively impacted her son. It caught her by complete surprise. Because she loved Jack and wanted to have a thriving relationship with him, she honored his request. Now, Jack knows exactly where to draw the line. When conversations are getting too heavy and overwhelm builds up, he lets his mom know, and the conversation changes course.

Ever since he's created those boundaries, his relationship with himself and his mom has improved tremendously. He and his mom laugh and enjoy each other so much more. They're now sharing more uplifting conversations instead of these heavy and dark conversations around what his mom was experiencing. Knowing that boundaries are an important part of his life now, Jack makes it a point to create new boundaries in all his relationships to have more peace of mind in his day-to-day interactions. This has resulted in him trading feelings of sadness, frustration, anxiety, and depression into feelings of peace, joy, and fulfillment. Creating boundaries has been a game-changer in his life.

 ### What You Can Stop Doing

Stop ruining your relationships because of a lack of boundaries. Stop making assumptions about what the other person "should know" or should do.

 ### What You Can Start Doing

Create clear boundaries with the people in your life.

 ### How You Can 2

Get clear on what is acceptable and not acceptable with each person in your life, including your partner, family, friends, and coworkers. Understand why this boundary is important for you. Once you know your boundaries and feel clear about them, communicate them with the people it will impact. Be ready to enforce boundaries, preferably when you are calm, not emotional charged.

Chapter 8: A Passion For Compassion

"Compassion and tolerance are not a sign
of weakness, but a sign of strength."
- Dalai Lama

It is the summer of 2012. I've been living at home with my mom and my brother now for about a year. While I'm standing in the kitchen, looking around, trying to find something to eat, my mom yells from her room, "Can you pick up my medicine from Walgreens?" I gasped, took a deep breath, and tried to control myself from getting angry. I replied, "Mom, I told you an hour ago that I'll go get it. Why do you keep asking me the same questions over and over again?" She laments, "You know I always forget. I'm losing my memory!" In frustration, I respond, "Mom, why would you say that? If you keep telling yourself that you're going to make it true."

My mom frequently asked my brother and me the same question multiple times, or she would tell us to do something multiple times, rarely remembering that she had already asked us. We never understood why. It is now apparent to me that she was starting to develop early signs of mental degeneration. Maybe it was early-onset Alzheimer's or something like that.

Alzheimer's is very much regarded as type three diabetes. Many of the same lifestyle factors and metabolic problems that we see in people with type two diabetes are going on to have Alzheimer's or dementia as they get older. Whenever my mom would repeatedly ask me a question or make a request, I immediately got frustrated. It was difficult for me to understand why she kept asking me the same question repeatedly. In my mind, she was annoying. In her mind, she was asking for the first time.

We came to notice that, again, her health was declining due to many of the lifestyle choices that she made throughout her life. Reflecting on these experiences, I realized I didn't have much compassion for my mom. Instead of understanding that her mental health was deteriorating, having compassion for her, and being there for her, I would be impatient and aggravated. What could have been more effective was remaining calm when she explained something to me for the tenth time. My frustration wasn't only with her early-onset Alzheimer's that showed up but also with her consistent lack of wellness.

As a child, I used to get mad at my mom when she couldn't take me somewhere. My mom was often too sick to go to my baseball games or take me to practice. I had no idea what she was going through; I only knew that I felt pain by her absence and extended no compassion to her. For years I was ignorant of how much pain she was in and how that pain prevented her from living a great life and physically being there for my brother and me. My mom was in some pain every single day. Her pain drove her to reach for pain medications daily, whether it was OxyContin or something else.

Unfortunately, using these types of medications numbed her so much that it knocked her out. She would be sleeping, or at least I thought she was asleep, for hours upon hours, and sometimes even days at a time. I remember thinking that my mom was lazy and avoiding everything that would help her get better. They always say hindsight is

20/20. My mom was stuck in a vicious cycle. The cycle starts with pain caused by lifestyle: lack of activity, eating processed foods, rancid vegetable oils, factory-farmed meat, and TV dinners. A life where she was pretty much immobile, not walking regularly, not swimming, not going outside for fresh air and sunlight. Deep breaths are replaced by shallow (and often) mouth breathing. The pain caused by lifestyle factors then led her to seek medications that would do their best to mask all of the symptoms without addressing the root cause. This is what the normal western healthcare (sick care) system does. It focuses on taking care of people's symptoms, but it doesn't address the root causes. The medication then causes a slew of painful side effects we've all heard about on TV commercials as they play beautiful music and show a couple falling in love. And the cycle of pain goes around and around.

From childhood through high school, I was unaware of how dissatisfied my mom was with her life. I was aloof to the amount of pain she was in physically, mentally, and emotionally. Overall, I was unaware of how truly sick she was. Some of my most vivid memories were of her constantly going to the bathroom, sitting there for hours, literally hours sitting on the toilet, because of all the gastric distress she had.

As a little boy in elementary school, I remember thinking that if I had the same type of stomach aches, maybe I'd take some of the pain away from my mom. Low and behold, very soon after having these thoughts, I had gastric distress too. As an elementary school student, I, too, would be on the toilet for 20 or 30 minutes at a time. This was my way of trying to take on my mom's pain. It was me trying to do something about her suffering, trying to alleviate some of her pain and take it on myself. It doesn't work like that. My poor health as a child manifested from trying to relieve her pain and suffering.

Fast forward to my adulthood, especially after I graduated from college and started living with her at home, I was the complete opposite. Instead of trying to take on her pain, I was disgusted by it. All the medications she took, all the horrible food she ate, the victim mentality that she had, the words she said to herself, the words she said to my brother and me, I looked at it all with real disdain. I honestly thought it was pathetic.

My frustration continued to build because I felt that she did not want to make any changes to improve her life. I went from having a martyr complex as a child to alleviate her pain to inflecting more pain onto her with my terrible attitude and judgement. What I lacked was compassion. Not once during those times did I look at my mom's circumstances from a bird's eye view to see all the pain my mom was in. If I had looked at her through the eyes that I look through today, I would have held so much more space for her. There would have been more action to meet her where she was to help her feel better. We would have collaborated and seen what I could do to help her help herself. What type of commitments would she be willing to make to herself to get better? Rather than taking her self-destructive actions personally, I would have sat there with compassion and said to myself, "Wow. The person that I love the most is hurting and in so much pain. She may not be ready to do something about it now, but when she is ready, I'll be here to help her to the best of my capabilities."

I can see how all my anger, pain, frustration, and dissatisfaction were present in my life because I lacked compassion. I often used my own experiences and compared them to others, thinking of what I would do if I were in her shoes. But I wasn't in her shoes. There was no way for me to feel the same pain and agony that she was feeling within my own body. Because of that, I underestimated how easy it would be for her to change. Unrealistically, I believed with a quick snap of the finger, she'd be able to pick herself up and start making some huge improvements in her lifestyle right away.

As I was going through my growth journey, I realized the positive actions I was taking in my life ultimately shifted the way I felt. Inspired, I thought to myself, "My mom can do all of these things too. If she eats better and exercises, she's going to feel better." But she wasn't ready for that yet. She wasn't mentally or emotionally prepared to take those steps for herself. Since I lacked compassion for how she was living her life, I would get angry, treating her disrespectfully in the process. In turn, she would yell at me and get more upset. This led to so much tension between the two of us.

Rehashing these memories still brings me pain. If I had a little bit of compassion for my mom, maybe she would still be alive today. One of my favorite definitions of compassion comes from Michael Bernard Beckwith. He explains that compassion is understanding that somebody else does not understand. I understand that my mom didn't understand how she was self-sabotaging. My mom didn't understand that the way she was eating, medicating, not moving, and overall, not taking care herself, made her feel much worse.

This was a vicious cycle. However, I didn't understand that she didn't understand that. Through my lack of understanding, it turned into me treating my mom horribly. I had a lot of resentment towards her for not doing things the way I wanted her to. Ultimately, this lack of compassion led to the anger and rage I showed her and to us not having the loving relationship that I now know I could have created with my mom.

My strained relationship with my mom showed me how important the role compassion plays in my world. Compassion is a foundational part of my life now. It is a principle that I follow every single day. Compassion, to me, is meeting people where they're at any given moment. It's important because it creates a space of understanding and allows me to practice empathy or sympathy in any given situation. Therefore, I don't judge others or label them. With everything going on in my world, I understand that every person around me is living their individual lives, going through their own specific experience. As a result, I don't let my perspective dictate how I treat them. I do my best to create a space where I'm meeting that person where they are, understanding that anything they do or say is never personal to me. It's simply a reflection of where they are.

This is an important lesson that I teach to all my clients: have compassion, be compassionate. Not only compassion for the people around them but also have compassion for themselves. In my own life I was the biggest asshole to myself in my own life, especially after my mom passed away. There is nothing someone else can say to me that is as horrible as what I told myself, all from a place of judgement and lack of compassion. For a few years after my mom's death, I beat myself up because I was disgusted with my relationship with my mom when she died. It took me several years to work through that trauma. A huge catalyst in working through that pain had compassion for my mom and myself, understanding that I was doing the best that I could at that time—also knowing that my mom was doing the best that she could at that time as well.

Throughout my professional career as a coach, I've had many clients who beat themselves up for getting to specific points of their lives that they were unhappy with. Through deep conversations, I'd help them understand and see how they were doing the best that they could at that given time. It's so easy to beat ourselves up. It's a lot harder to show grace and have compassion for ourselves when our expectations for ourselves are so damn high all the time.

My client, Todd, was a great example of this. Before we started working together, Todd was trending towards taking blood pressure medication because of his lifestyle choices. He called me in hopes of improving all his blood markers so that he wouldn't need to get on blood pressure medication. Todd had been an athlete all his life. He loved being active, playing basketball, exercising, and running around with his kids when they were younger. As an entrepreneur operating a business with his wife, he slowly started to let himself go. He put his business and his family ahead of his well-being. This resulted in him eating poorly, sleeping little, not exercising, and being heavily stressed, all of which led to his blood markers being in a place where his doctor told him he was going to need to make some significant lifestyle changes or else he would need to be put on statin drugs.

This was a huge wake-up call for Todd. He did not want to depend on medications. We sat down and took inventory of the many aspects of his life. I challenged him to assess how he was currently eating, hydrating, sleeping, exercising, breathing, and thinking. It did not take much time for him to realize that he had a lot of work to do to change his fate.

We decided to start with exercise and nutrition. As we started getting deeper into exercise and training in the gym together three times per week, we built trust and rapport. This bond that we were building allowed us to have deeper conversations regarding his life. We dove deeper into his lifestyle and where his stress was coming from. What Todd started to uncover was how hard he was on himself all the time.

He was beating himself up for choices that he made years ago. Instead of leaving those thoughts in the past, he was bringing them with him everywhere he went. He didn't realize that this way of thinking about himself and beating himself up consistently was causing immense amounts of stress in his life.

The body doesn't know the difference between physical stress, mental stress, or emotional stress. The body interprets stress as stress. The body's reaction is the same; it will cause inflammation and all types of metabolic deficiencies throughout. Once Todd realized how hard he was on himself and that it was negatively impacting his health, we began to unpack the concept of compassion. He started to show himself grace. He did the inner work of uncovering what his thought processes were in the past that caused him to stress and be so hard on himself. He searched within himself to see if, during those times, he was doing his best to get a great result. Upon deeply reflecting and coming from a neutral place, he realized that the truth of the matter was that he was doing his best. He was doing his best in all those situations to create a great result.

But at the time, that was not the way he was thinking about it. Instead, everything that he was doing was not "good enough." He didn't realize how ineffective his thought patterns were. These thought patterns led to ineffective actions. It wasn't that his intentions were bad, but the mechanisms were not working. The way he was going about it was not working. By seeing it that way, he started to have more compassion for himself. He intentionally worked on being gentle when he made a mistake or when something did not go his way. Before he knew it, a huge weight was lifted from his shoulders. While we were working together, he would make mistakes and do things that would frustrate him, but he could tap into compassion quickly, which prevented his stress levels from accumulating.

He created new systems for processing stress. When things got tough in his life, he developed the habit of asking himself, "Okay, what's the new action I get to take that's effective and takes me where I want to go? What is going to be the most successful way of thinking that is going to allow me to get out of this rut and make better decisions?" Ever since Todd has incorporated compassion into his life, his stress levels have gone way down, his mental and emotional clarity have gone up, and I am proud to say that Todd never had to go on those statin drugs. He is in the best physical, mental, and emotional shape of his life.

 What You Can Stop Doing

Stop taking what other people do and say personally.

 What You Can Start Doing

Have compassion for yourself and others.

 How You Can 2

Understand that anything that someone else says or does reflects them, not a reflection of who you are. Have compassion for yourself by knowing that you are not perfect and will make mistakes. Do your best to learn from each of these mistakes and grow from them. Have compassion for others by realizing that they are human and have their ups and downs in life. Most people are doing their best with what they know.

Chapter 9: Celebrate YOU

"The more you praise and celebrate your life,
the more there is in life to celebrate."
- Oprah Winfrey

It's November of 2019. I'm in a transformational leadership development program located in South Florida. I participated in the program because I felt it was the next step to becoming the best version of myself physically, emotionally, mentally, and spiritually. At the time, there were many skills and gifts in my arsenal that I was bringing into the world. But I felt like I was still holding back in different parts of my life, specifically in unleashing my full potential when using my voice for change and stepping into my power.

The program that I participated in was composed of three distinct parts. Part one was geared towards finding where my blind spots were. It was a four-day training focused on shedding light on the thoughts, words, and actions that were not serving me and ultimately had me play small. Awareness of self was key here. Part one allowed me to take all that I had learned up to that point through my personal experiences and the knowledge I gained from different personal development teachings and apply it through experiential learning. Experiential means that I was using these learnings through real situations with others, not through theory alone. This is kind of like driving a car. You can study everything there is no know about driving, but until you get behind the wheel and drive the car, you'll never know what the experience is like.

Part two focused on breaking through those blind spots over a five-day, sixty-hour period. Once I was aware of these blind spots, part two allowed me to learn tangible tools to overcome them. The exercises throughout part two put me in a position to stretch my comfort zone, challenge my thoughts, be vulnerable, and courageously take action when it came to leading myself and the other 48 people on my team.

Part three was a three-month program focused on creating mastery around these breakthroughs in all aspects of my life, including career, health, relationships, leisure time, personal growth, spiritual growth, and community. We collaborated on an extensive community project while simultaneously creating individual goals for our own lives as a group. The transformation I experienced during the entire program spanned a total of five months. Within these five months, I consistently had revelations regarding how my past experiences shaped how I was showing up in the world today.

The experiential learning component of this program was a game-changer for me. Within experiential learning, we engaged in different exercises that allowed us to receive feedback. This was an interesting experience because I've received feedback my entire life, but I never evaluated my relationship with feedback. One exercise hit me hard. We were instructed to give feedback to each team member in our group of 49, including ourselves. The feedback be given in the form of voting yes or no. A "yes" vote would indicate that in the hypothetical situation, where only five people in the room survived, would they be someone I vote for to live. Intense, I know. The rules were that we could only vote for five people, and we could vote for ourselves.

During this feedback process, I was selected into the top five based on the number of votes I received from everybody. The people with the most votes were told to sit in chairs in the middle of the room. I started walking over to the chairs. Then I hear the trainer yell, "if you did not vote for yourself, you could not sit in the chair." Oops, there was my problem. I did not vote myself. I voted for others but didn't vote for myself to lead if it came down to five surviving people.

Since I didn't vote for myself, I couldn't be considered one of the top five. Even after finding out that I was not going to be considered for the top five, I wasn't upset. I didn't care. In my mind, it was just a stupid game. It didn't matter; I was voted top five anyway.

However, my feelings soon changed. At the end of this exercise, all the people who didn't make it into the top five were going to be delivering their last messages ever to their loved ones. It was up to the people in the top five, the five people with the most votes and who also voted to save themself, to share those messages for them. I was lying down on the floor with my eyes closed, with everyone else wasn't selected, while the other top five were sitting up in chairs listening.

After I yelled out my last words that I would pass on to my loved ones, I relaxed onto the floor, listening with open ears and an open heart to see what came up. I was shook to my core as I heard a dozen different people yell out my name. "Alvey, tell my daughter I love them and that I will miss them so much." A man shouted, "Alvey, tell my mom that I will always be with her." Another woman yelled, "Alvey, tell my husband and son that I think about them every day." As I took in all these messages, I started sobbing. I couldn't believe that even though I wasn't selected, people were still thinking about me and wanted me to share those messages with them.

After the exercise and leaving the training center that night, I sat with myself and reflected on this exercise and why the experience had me emotionally shaken. I connected the dots and saw how not voting for myself was a common theme in my life. I never took the time to acknowledge myself. As I started to dig deeper into that and think about where that came from, I was brought back to a specific moment in my childhood.

When I was 11-years-old, my life was very simple. I enjoyed playing competitive baseball, playing outside with my friends, watching sports, and playing video games. In school, I was one of the more popular kids, best athletes, and best students. Even though I had a lot of good things going on for me at the time, I never thought any of it was a big deal. On the other hand, my mom believed it was news that the whole world needed to hear. She was so proud to be my mom. This showed up in every conversation I ever heard her have as I was a young boy growing up.

I would always overhear my mom's phone conversations with her friends and family. Much of my mom's life at that point was spent on her bed in the house. She never went out because she always felt too sick. You can't have much of a social life if you don't leave your house, so all her interactions with others took place over the phone.

Every single day, I would hear her rehashing the same conversations repeatedly, multiple times a day. During those times, a huge part of those conversations would always revolve around me. My mom would say, "Danny's doing so good in school; he's making the best grades. He's one of the smartest kids in his class. He's doing great at baseball; he hit another home run this weekend. He's one of the best players on his team. Danny's so handsome. He's growing up so fast. I can tell that all the girls like him."

She would consistently brag about me. On this specific day in the fifth grade, I remember hearing my mom brag about me in her usual delighted fashion while walking from my bedroom to the kitchen. She again talked about how smart I was, how good-looking I was, how great I was at sports, and how I excelled in all these areas of my life.

Instantly, I felt this wave of embarrassment run through my entire body. I was timid at that time of my life. Hearing my mom say these things repeatedly made me feel incredibly uncomfortable. So uncomfortable that I built up a defense mechanism where any praise I listened to my mom say would go in one ear and directly out the other. But I wasn't aware that this defense mechanism was formed or stayed with me for literally the rest of my life.

From that time in fifth grade up until that specific exercise in this training program, where I was a 31-year-old man, I realized the extent to which I blocked out all acknowledgment and praise that came my way. By this time, I was deep into my career as a holistic life coach, a personal trainer, and a sports performance trainer. Hundreds of people's physical, mental, emotional, and spiritual health have been transformed by my work. My resume included helping dozens of youth athletes become starters for their high school team, dozens of high school athletes go from high school starter to receiving a college scholarship to play their sport, having college athletes go from the college ranks into the pros, and helping pros level-up and become starters on their professional team.

My work also included helping single mothers, just like my mom, gain confidence, appreciate their bodies, and love themselves for who they are. I helped hundreds of people in my time, yet, with the hundreds of times I heard "thank you" and the appreciation others showed me, I blocked it all out. It would come in one ear and flow right out the other.

This resulted in me not having an appreciation for myself. I did not see myself as worthy of the prices that I wanted to charge in my practice. It made me see myself as not worthy of going after the super high-performing clients I was already attracting and working with. It created a strong sense of self-doubt within me. All that doubt and imposter syndrome that I was putting on myself resulted in me playing small in the world. I was living way under my potential.

That experience helped me realize at that moment as a fifth-grader, when I started to block everything out, I began the process of robbing myself of the abundance of opportunity that was always around me. I can see how it resulted in me showing up small during my high school career, how I wasn't building the relationships that I wanted to build, that I wasn't going after the romantic relationships that I truly wanted in high school, college, or as a young adult.

It showed up in my college football career. Even though I had a Division I scholarship to play at Georgetown, I was always afraid to make a mistake on the field. All because I didn't acknowledge the natural abilities that I've shown for years. The abilities that allowed me to receive this scholarship in the first place. Even after I graduated from Georgetown, whenever a conversation came up about where I went to school, I would say that I went to school in DC. I wouldn't even name Georgetown, which is so silly when I look at it now.

I realized that I was embarrassed to say that because I wasn't worthy of that school. That I wasn't worthy enough to recognize myself as a Georgetown alumnus, even though all my hard work in the classroom and on the field allowed me to graduate on time in four years. It's so interesting because I realized that this all stems from a lack of self-acknowledgement. Because I wasn't acknowledging myself or congratulating myself, I wasn't showing up as powerfully as I could in the world.

My biggest lesson from all of this is that I get to accept praise. When somebody tells me, "Thank you," when someone tells me how much I've impacted their life when someone is telling me how good I am at what I do, or how my words have inspired them, I now get to bring that into my body, feel it, and embrace it. I get to allow all the positive emotions to run through my body. I get to embody the emotions of happiness, pride, appreciation, and gratitude because I now whole-heartedly understand that I am making an incredible impact on other people, and most of all, on myself. Now that I acknowledge to myself how I make an incredible impact on the lives of others, I take the time every single day to celebrate myself. I celebrate my wins, no matter how small. I take the time to congratulate myself when I accomplish a big goal. I take the time to bring in and cherish the praise that other people are giving me instead of just letting it go in one ear and out the other.

I realize how important this is because, in the same way, I must fill my cup; it's also essential that I'm my biggest cheerleader and recognize myself for my greatness. Recognizing my excellence allows me to build the momentum to continue taking courageous action towards my goals and achieving my dream life. It was so strange that it took me damn nearly twenty years to realize that I was holding myself small because I was not accepting praise. All because I was embarrassed as a young child of how much my mom would celebrate me. Of course, my mom would celebrate with me; that's what moms do! Of course, she's going to be so happy and joyous for everything that I accomplished. Today I'm grateful for that.

When it comes to my clients, I work as hard as possible to help them acknowledge themselves. The first thing we do before every session goes over their wins for the week. What are you most proud of? I give my client the time to celebrate himself and realize that he is doing great things for himself, others, and the world. The acknowledgement of every single win allows momentum to build up. As each win is counted, and they see all of these wins compiling, that turns into energy to keep moving forward. They continually prove what they are capable of and use this as concrete evidence to keep showing up for themselves in a powerful way. One of my good friends, Tom, is a great example of this. Tom and I had the pleasure of working together for over a year. Tom was very similar to me in that he never wanted to give himself credit. If I complimented him on how he looked because he lost some weight, he would say, "Oh no, it's the shirt. Black is always slimming." Every time I would congratulate him on creating a goal, taking action, and completing it, he would explain, "I'm just doing what I'm supposed to do." This was him completely downplaying his greatness. This was a common theme in his life. As his coach, I would bring it to his awareness in any situation where he would downplay himself like that. I would ask, "Can you see how you are keeping yourself small again? Here you go, not acknowledging yourself for the amazing things that you're doing. How can you have gratitude and appreciation for what you're achieving if you're not willing to celebrate yourself?"

Slowly over time, he started to recognize how his lack of self-acknowledgment directly contributed to his lack of action on his most important goal: improving his relationship with himself. Upon correlating how increased self-acknowledgement can improve his relationship with himself, he committed to making changes. Tom decided he was ready to work on celebrating himself. Week after week, he would celebrate his wins with more and more enthusiasm. When we first started celebrating his wins, it was very embarrassing for him. It felt strange; it was out of his comfort zone. He was so used to being humble, even though he used humility to disguise self-doubt. But once we got a few weeks into it, that discomfort turned into enthusiasm.

He would have a big smile from ear to ear about what he had

accomplished during the previous week. Those accomplishments would lead to bigger accomplishments down the road. It all stemmed from him having a better relationship with himself by acknowledging himself and the achievements that he was creating in his life. Now he lives a life where he realizes that celebrating himself and acknowledging the work he puts in is not bragging. It is personal recognition. This level of recognition allowed him to embody how worthy he is, love himself deeply, and have the confidence to go out and create his Dream Life. Always vote for yourself.

 ## What You Can Stop Doing

Stop letting all your achievements go by without taking the time to acknowledge them and deeply appreciate them.

 ## What You Can Start Doing

Start consistently acknowledging all the wins you've obtained and deeply appreciate the journey it took to get there.

 ## How You Can 2

Write down all your wins, no matter how big or small. Write them down at the end of each night and keep them in a file altogether. You can do this on your computer or in your notebook; make sure you have them in a place that is easy to find. Whenever you are feeling down, pull these out and read them to yourself to remind you of how powerful you are!

Chapter 10: Trauma Spreads Like Wildfire

"Hurt people hurt people."
- Anonymous

It was June 2015, just a few weeks after one of the most incredible people in my life died. My grandfather, aka Pop, passed away from heart complications. This was a difficult time for everybody in the family. Pop was the man. My dad wasn't around that much when I was growing up, but I never felt the presence of a father figure in my life because I had Pop. When I was a child, Pop would pick me up from school every two weeks and take me out on "my day." Pop had six grandchildren, including me, and each of us had our designated day with him, where it was just 1:1 quality time. My day was my opportunity to go out, play, and have a good time. He would take me to places like Dave and Busters, the movie theater, or to the park to play football. Whatever my heart desired that day, Pop would make it happen. Me and my cousins, still talk about it to this day. He made us feel special by meeting with each of us and doing what we desired to do.

Pop was also at every one of my sporting events. He made it to 90% of my games from T-ball through my senior year of high school football. Pop was in the stands at every single game, cheering me on.

He was the best example of unconditional love that I have ever experienced in my life up to date. He loved me no matter what. There were many occasions where I would be a huge brat, driving my brother crazy in the process. Pop would never get in between my brother and me. He would never scold me or scold him when we were bickering boys.

My love of nature, the sun, and the outdoors come from Pop. He moved from New Jersey to South Florida so that he could be in the sun. He was in the sun so much that most people thought Pop, a white man, was my dad. That's my mom's dad. He's a white man. Yet, everyone thought he was my dad because of how dark he was.

Pop was the type of person who would beat the sun to the beach, using the sunrise as the time to lather himself in all of the suntan oil he could get his hands on. He would lay out there to bronze until the sun went down. The beach was his sanctuary. My uncle, Scott, shared a story with me that perfectly captures Pop's love for the sun. One day Pop was at his house and somehow ran out of his tanning oil. Not to be deterred, he found another solution. He walked to the kitchen, reached up into the cabinet, and pulled out a bottle of Crisco cooking oil. He proceeded to rub Crisco all over his body, sat outside on his favorite pool chair, and baked in the sun.

That's who my grandfather was. He also prided himself on his physical fitness. He exercised and lifted weights well into his 70s until his doctor eventually told him to lay off. Even with that ultimatum, he still snuck some bicep curls in every week. Pop is where I got my love for the sun and exercising. He is also directly responsible for my passion for football. Pop had been a football player from when he was a little kid through high school, where he was a star linebacker on his team. He was the biggest Miami Dolphins fan, consistently buying season tickets and taking a bunch of people from the family to the games.

Pop taught me the ins and outs of the game of football. He taught me what to look for when watching the games. How to study the line play, how to understand what was going on in coverage, and to appreciate the chess match that was going on between the two head coaches. I don't know if anything I did made him happier than when he discovered that I would finally start my football career in high school. He was ecstatic, making sure that he made it to every one of my games and even some practices, always ready to give me feedback on what I did well and how I could improve. Pop was always there for me. He was always there for everybody in our family. Everyone adored him. His grandchildren, children, and friends, everybody cherished Pop because he was an amazing, loving, and charismatic human being.

All our worlds turned upside down when he suddenly died. The entire family was devastated when he passed away from heart complications post-surgery. My household was in chaos because my mom, brother, and I felt like we had lost a huge piece of ourselves. Around this time, my brother and my mom had their fair share of health problems going on.

While my mom was making significant improvements in her lifestyle, she was still addicted to her pain medication. My brother, Hank, also developed an addiction to pain medication. About a year or two before Pop passed away; Hank broke his foot. His doctor prescribed him OxyContin for it. Over time, he eventually became addicted to it. This caused a substantial number of arguments between my mom and my brother.

For whatever reason, my mom, at times, would give my brother some of her OxyContin when he asked her for it. There were instances when my mom would count her pills and, according to her, the number would be off. But my mom's memory was horrible, and she would not be sure if she gave my brother some or if he stole it from her. You could bet that the majority of the time, she would jump to the conclusion that he stole her pills. This caused some of the most verbally abusive arguments I have ever heard in my life. These destructive arguments were a weekly occurrence in our home.

One day, I'm hanging out in my room, watching TV, when out of nowhere, a huge argument ensues between the two of them. This was just another day in my life. When this happened, I would hear it and be upset for a moment, but I would block it out for the most part. A few minutes into their argument, my ears perked up, and my eyes opened wide. I've heard my mom say some terrible things to my brother in the past, but this was taken to a new level of disgust. My mom yelled, "You should have fucking died! Not Pop!"

My heart sank. My blood boiled. I violently swung my door open. Before I could even see her, I yelled, "What the fuck is wrong with you? Why would you say something like that?" My mom looked directly into my eyes and stated, "I'm sick of him! He's a fucking liar! I want him out of my house!"

The ups and downs that my mom and brother experienced together were insane. They had an extremely codependent relationship. My mom depended on my brother to do everything for her. My brother was the one who would consistently pick up my mom's medications from the pharmacy. At that time, I was so fed up with how reliant my mom was on her medication that I said I wouldn't get them for her. I told myself that I wasn't going to aid her in taking that poison. That's where my mindset was at the time. My mom depended on my brother to get the groceries. At the time, I told my mom that I wasn't buying any food that was not in alignment with my food values, so I'd only buy my groceries.

My mom depended on my brother to do all the chores and those errands for her. In return, my brother got to live at home, almost rent-free. He paid very little to live there. Because he was living under her roof, my mom would treat him as if he was a little boy. The truth is that my mom treated Hank like a child the entire time she was alive. She was usually hard on him, rarely gave him words of affirmation, or gave him the space to grow as a man.

My perspective of Hank when I was little was that of adornment. Every day I wanted to hang out with him, throw the baseball or football around, and play video games together. Since he is seven years older than me, he rarely wanted me to be around him and his friends. I get it. Most older siblings don't want their snotty-nosed younger siblings to be around them. He wanted his space and autonomy. Since I wanted to be around him so much, I would annoy the hell out of him when he was not giving me the attention I yearned for. This typically led to some form of him picking on me, me crying to my mom, and then my mom punishing Hank. This caused Hank to have resentment towards me during his teenage years. He knew that my mom let me get away with various actions that he would get punished for. Most of their arguments when I was in elementary school revolved around how unfairly he was treated compared to me. This wasn't fair to Hank at all, but it was what it was. My mom favorably treated me compared to Hank and it led to a strained relationship between the three of us well into our adulthood.

At the point of this huge fight between my brother and mom, Hank was already in his early 30's. My brother was at the moment in his life where he always felt defeated when it came to my mom. After being broken down for years, he reached the point where he would rarely yell back. He would take it. He would endure the crazy things that my mom would say to him. Usually, I would try my best to stay out of it. But at this point, I couldn't hold back. I could not believe that my mom told my brother, her son, that she wished he had died instead of my grandfather. In my twenty-five years of life, I heard my mom say unforgivable words to my brother, but this was by far the worst. This caused me to explode, turn all of the focus on her failings as a mother, and say all types of shitty things to her in the process. All I saw was red. All I could think to myself was, "What type of a mother would tell their son that they wish he were dead?!"

This crazy situation put me in a dark place. I was hurting so much on the inside from all the turmoil in my life. Pop's death, hearing my mom say that she wished my brother was dead, and me telling my mom how terrible of a mother she has created a cloud of hate, anger, and sadness around me. I realized that the dynamic between my brother, my mom, and myself was abusive. It was considered an act of God for a week to go by without there being some form of verbal warfare between at least two of us. When it came to my brother and me, our arguments sometimes turned into physical altercations.

There was a long part of my life where my brother thought he had a physical and psychological edge over me. When I was little, he would beat me up, common in many brother relationships. I'm pretty sure a lot of that stemmed from jealousy because my mom would treat me much differently than she would treat him. I consistently got away with a lot more than he did. He often beat me up because I was being a brat little brother, antagonizing him, calling him names, and making fun of him. After all, I could get away with it. Many times, he would take his anger and frustration out on me. I never held a grudge against him for it, and I don't have a grudge against him today. Even though he still expresses to me up to this day that he thinks I do.

One day, during my junior year in high school, he tried to intimidate me. Being a 6'1, 240-pound football player at the time, I was not scared of him anymore. We got into one of our usual arguments, screaming and cussing at each other. He got in my face, I pushed him, he pushed me back, then I proceeded to wrestle him through one of the walls in my bedroom. As you can imagine, my mom was pissed off. This was the first time in my life I successfully stood up to my brother and won a fight between us. Unfortunately, this wasn't our last confrontation.

Fast forward about five years later; there was a time where Hank and I got into an argument about something stupid. I'm pretty sure he ate my food or something stupid like that. We started yelling at each other, testosterone levels rising, seeing who was going to punk who. It got to the point where I got behind him, yoked him up, and had my bicep pressed deep into Adam's apple, choking him out. My mom got so scared and upset that she pulled out a large steak knife, pointed it at me, and told me to let him go.

You can only imagine the chaos of that scene. My brother is in a headlock, my mom is pointing a knife towards me, and I'm a crazed lunatic, eyes-wide, face red, ready to put my brother to sleep. Reflecting on this madness, I realized how to hurt all of us were. All three of us lived lives that embodied rage and hate that could not be contained. What I learned from this is that hurt people hurt people. When I was there, choking my brother, it resulted in me deeply hurting mentally and emotionally. I was not well. When my mom told my brother that she wished that he had died instead of my grandfather, I knew that was because she was hurt. She was physically, mentally, emotionally, and spiritually sick. When a person is sick like that, they will do unforgivable things.

My brother didn't have a lot going on for him. He hated his job at the Cheesecake Factory, was addicted to his pain medicine, had a victim mentality, and lacked a social life. As a result, he, too, was hurting physically, mentally, emotionally, and spiritually. He would take that out on me and my mom through yelling and arguing. As I look at this triangle of chaos, pain, and unforgivable actions, I realize that it happened because all of us were hurt. Hurt people hurt people. After my mom's passing, I saw how prevalent this was in our life. It wasn't until after I started taking care of myself at a high level, not only eating well and exercising but by meditating, practicing gratitude, journaling, and other forms of inner work, did I start to heal these traumas.

Once I started healing, I felt better physically, emotionally, mentally, and spiritually, which prevented me from lashing out at people around me. Since I was no longer hurting immensely, I was no longer hurting others. Creating a sense of peace and staying grounded has shifted how I feel internally about myself and the world around me. Learning this lesson has become a foundational aspect of how I work with my clients. We collaborated in helping them realize that when they heal themselves, they end up healing the world around them. For us to heal this planet, it starts with each one of us healing ourselves first.

One of my previous clients, Kyle, was the type of person who was extremely hurt on the inside. He had a significant number of things happening in his life that caused pain, bitterness, and anger within him. When he was angry, he didn't feel like he was a good person. He would let his internal anger overflow into the relationships around him. His friendships were deteriorating, his relationship with his partner was barely holding on, and his relationship with his family was falling apart. To him, anything that wasn't working in his life was someone else's fault. He wasn't taking ownership and looking within.

First, I asked him, "What are some of the common denominators that you see in all of these deteriorating relationships that you have?" After pondering for some time, he realized that he was the common denominator in each one of these situations. He understood that he would inflict emotional pain on those around him when he was angry or hurt. It wasn't something he was doing consciously, yet it was frequently happening. Once he realized this pattern and decided that it was not serving him, he committed to making changes. He was ready to do the necessary work on himself. We focused on energy management. He began to take breathing breaks throughout his day, focusing on taking ten deep breaths through the nose and out through the mouth. During the first week, he performed this three times per day. Once in the morning before work, once after lunch, and again at the end of the workday. Over eight weeks, those ten breaths turned into 20, then 20 turned into 50, And before he knew it, he was formally meditating for thirty minutes at a time. The first thing he noticed was how he could feel himself calm down. He developed the ability to catch himself being angry and upset. From there, he started to learn what his specific triggers were that got him this way.

Upon realizing what those triggers were, we co-created tangible ways to work on them. Over time, by noticing these triggers, working on them, and understanding that they were there to teach him something, he felt his anger diminish. With the ability to control his anger, he saw his relationships with his partner, family, and friends improve.

Now he utilizes the following process any time he's feeling angry or upset:

He identifies what was that triggering event.

He checks in and sees what feelings are coming up for him.

He notices what his thoughts are around these feelings.

He decides the actions he's going to take based on those thoughts and feelings.

He asks himself what the results are that he's going to generate.

Lastly, he sees if the results he developed serve him.

He is more grounded and has a tremendous amount of peace in his life by going through that process.

 What You Can Stop Doing

Stop taking your anger, sadness, frustration, or any other negative emotions out on others.

 What You Can Start Doing

Work on healing your traumas.

 How You Can 2

First, realize that there are personal issues that you are going through that need to be worked on for the better. From this place of awareness, commit to getting help through a professional that you trust and do your inner work. Inner work includes but is not limited to: journaling, meditating, breathwork, reflecting, and introspecting. Become aware of how you are feeling and decide to take action to change for the better.

Chapter 11: Forgiveness Is Freedom

"Forgiveness is for yourself because it frees you. It lets
you out of that prison you put yourself in."
- Louise Hay

On my 29th birthday, October 11, 2017, I had one of the most profound experiences of my life. I finished watching the University of Miami vs. FSU rivalry football game at a local bar in Fort Lauderdale. We celebrated all day long at the beach doing the things I love: being around my friends, enjoying the saltwater, the sand, the sun, and the weather overall. After the football game, one of my best friends meets us and has a bunch of psilocybin mushrooms on him.

Up to this point, I had heard about psilocybin on different podcasts that I listened to. In all the different episodes I listened to, there were a sizable number of positive effects that participants experienced. It was helping these individuals heal from previous traumas, improve their relationships, and increase their levels of well-being. I had never had the chance to experience it, and based on the information I heard, I was very interested in experiencing this powerful medicine. When my friend showed up and offered to facilitate the experience for me, it was a no-brainer. I was a HELL YES!

These were some of the most memorable six hours of my life. My first psilocybin journey was shared with three of my closest friends. We were in his apartment, which was a very safe space, enabling me to feel comfortable. At first, I didn't notice anything. My three friends were talking about their experiences, laughing, and having a great time. I closed my eyes for a moment. Very soon after shutting my eyes, I felt my heart burst open. A flood of positive emotions washed over my body, creating a huge smile on my face from ear to ear. I felt like a kid again, super happy for no specific reason. I remember thinking to myself, "I can't remember the last time I experienced this level of pure joy. What the hell is this?!" Instead of trying to make sense of it all, I decided to surrender to the experience and allow it to take me wherever I was meant to go. Being able to let go in this way allowed me to have an insightful experience throughout the night.

All three of us were laughing, telling stories, and genuinely enjoying the present moment. While we talked about anything that came up, we also took time to go within, allowing me to be introspective. During this time of self-reflection, I uncovered things about myself, formed different perspectives around life, developed new conclusions, and viewed my life through a new lens. This night opened a door of new possibilities for me. My curiosity peaked. I was ready to see how these powerful plant medicines could create a beneficial impact in my life. I was unsure of what this journey would look like, yet I knew it was going to help me level up immensely.

In January of 2018, I went to my favorite beach spot in Dania Beach, Florida. It was a gorgeous sunny day, partially cloudy, with a cool breeze. My intention for the trip was to be outside by myself, eat mushrooms, dare to dive deep within my emotions, and be open to whatever feelings came up. Very soon after ingesting the mushrooms, I was in euphoria. I was smiling, laughing, dancing, playing in the sand and water, just appreciating how marvelous my life was. The medicine had me in a deep state of gratitude for doing work that I loved, hanging out with people I loved, eating good, exercising, and feeling great about my mind, body, spirit, and soul.

About an hour into my experience, there was a moment where the wind picked up and started swirling. This whole time I was by myself, not a person in sight. Soon after the wind slowed down, I noticed someone was there with me. It was my mom's presence. Somehow, someway, my mom joined me in my experience at the beach. Instantly, I began thinking about her, and I felt thrilled that we were sharing our first moment in over two years. It was a beautiful moment. This was the first time I could feel this amount of love, joy, and peace with my mom. I couldn't believe that I was with her. The amount of gratitude and appreciation I had at that moment showed me how much I missed my mom and how deeply I loved her.

Suddenly, in a flash, an enormous gray cloud came over the sun, turning everything dark. A strong, cold breeze ran through my body, immediately bringing me to tears. I could feel that my mom was gone and no longer there with me at the beach. This made me as sad as the day she passed away. Shocked, I couldn't believe how quickly I went from experiencing euphoria, and unconditional love, from being with my mom to all of it being gone.

In the blink of an eye, with one gust of the wind, that moment was gone. It was eerily reminiscent of how I felt when I found out that my mom would die. I sat there with myself, genuinely allowing myself the opportunity to heal through the crying, sadness, and introspection. Deep in my heart, I know that I grew massively that day. Soon after being in that place of sadness, I returned to smiling, being joyous, and happy for having that special moment with my mom at the beach. I walked away from this experience with a tremendous amount of happiness and appreciation for where my life was and my mom's impact on my life.

This entire experience got leveled up tenfold when I went on my first ayahuasca retreat six months before my 30th birthday. During the Spring of 2018, by the luck of how my life was going and the universe having me in the right places at the right time, I had the opportunity to do ayahuasca in Austin, Texas. I was welcomed by an extraordinary group of shamans who brought me into their home and opened a sacred space for 18 of us to dive deep within ourselves. On the very first night of this three-night journey, I'm positioned directly next to the mesa. The mesa is the table where all the sacred objects used to improve the energy of the space are placed. I intentionally sat right next to the shamans. After consuming the ancient tea, I remember feeling extremely anxious, waiting for the medicine to kick in.

About 45 minutes after consuming the medicine, I finally began to relax, surrender and have patience for the process. When the ayahuasca encompassed my being, I felt so much joy and jubilation. The first thing I did was go one by one down a list of all my friends and family, see their faces, and begin sending them love. They all deserved to know how much I loved and appreciated them, and the impact they had on my life. It was a nourishing yet powerful moment.

During the entire ceremony, it was difficult for me to comprehend how much time had gone by. Fast forward into the night, and I found myself lying on my side, thinking about Pop. A split-second into bringing him into my awareness, I had a huge explosion of love fill my entire being. Before I knew it, I was in the fetal position on my mat in my blanket. Instantly, I was reminded of an experience that felt all too familiar to me. I just re-entered my mom's womb. While in this position, I started to remember many loving, heart-warming moments that my mom and I shared. All these memories that I had blocked out for years were now flooding into my nervous system. My brain now remembered all the impactful events and moments my mom created in my life.

We didn't have a lot of money growing up. But somehow, my mom provided the most magical, legendary Christmas mornings ever. Every year she would find a way to get the number one thing on the list and somehow surprise me with it. While lying on my mat, I went through every Christmas I had with my mom and brother. Memories of my mom attending all the sporting events that she did make it to. She always made sure that I could play the sport, afford the nicest equipment, or get scholarships and sponsorships to make sure that I was able to participate.

As a 29-year-old, that was the first time I could truly see the unconditional love my mom showed me. Never in my entire life had it been as apparent as in that moment that my mom did any and everything to make sure that I was taken care of. The love and appreciation I had for my mom was breathtaking.

At that moment, I acknowledged that I got my love for being in service to others from my mom. My desire to help others came by seeing all the ineffective and inefficient ways she lived her life while alive. My mom's ways of helping others were self-defeating because they constantly came at her own expense. Her death taught me how important it is to make sure that I'm first taking care of myself at the highest level possible to help others truly. The terrible ways I treated my mom when she wasn't making the changes I thought she should make inspired me to learn to meet people and harness compassion. These epiphanies led me to realize that my mom played a monumental role in the way I was helping myself and others live the best life possible.

Before this specific moment, on my mat, in my mom's womb, I had always told myself that it didn't matter how many people I helped. The hundreds of athletes, from the youth to professional ranks, the countless moms, executives, lawyers, and high performers that I've helped, did not matter in the grand scheme of things. It didn't matter to me because, in the end, I couldn't help the person that I loved the most, my mom.

I named my company YouCan2 because I always heard my mom say, "I can't." I would ask, "Mom, why don't you eat this thing?" She would lament, "I can't." "Why don't you go to this place?" "I can't." She had a fixed mindset. She believed that she was not able to change certain things about herself. As a result, she continually looked outside of herself to go and find fulfillment.

I had looked at my business from this dark place. It came from this story I told myself where everything I accomplished was insufficient, and I was unworthy of any praise I received because I couldn't help my mom. Yet, at that moment, I learned my biggest lesson of all time, forgiveness is for myself, not others. At that moment, lying on the mat, I forgave my mom for deciding to get the surgery. I forgave the doctor, who agreed that he would do the surgery, even though he knew that my mom was not healthy enough to have that surgery. I forgave the ineffective system that had my mom being taken care of by twelve independent doctors and specialists, who all saw her coma from their very small lens. They weren't collaborative. They never had answers when my family and I were on our weekly visits.

I forgave all of them. Most importantly, I forgave myself for how I treated my mom from when I graduated college in 2011 until her death in May of 2015. Forgiveness was given for all the arguments, my lack of gratitude and appreciation for her, yelling and cussing at her, not talking to her for weeks on end, and not giving her the satisfaction of knowing what was going on in my life. I'd been beating myself up mercilessly about those dozens of experiences for the last three years.

I decided to forgive myself, shifting my mindset to see that the things I wanted my mom to change came from a place of love. I had compassion for myself, realizing that I didn't have an effective way to express my sentiments so that my mom could feel my love. I did not create a space where my mom could receive my suggestions from a place of love and still allow her to decide for herself. From that same place of love, I would accept any decision she made.

All these life-altering insights were a result of only my very first night. Sitting with the medicine that first night has been, hands down, the most pivotal moment in my healing journey. What I've learned about forgiveness is that forgiveness is always for me. Forgiveness allows me to release the stressful weight from a given trauma and move forward in my life in a dream affirmative way. I was beating myself up so much about my mom's death and my way of being during that time that it had me play small. I didn't believe that I deserved to have amazing things. I didn't think that I deserved to train and be paid by some of the best athletes in the world.

I trained Michael Vick for four months one offseason when people thought his NFL playing career was made. This is a person who had been through so much adversity, was so polarizing, and one of the biggest names in sports history. I'm so grateful that I got to learn what an incredible man he is. He was a living example of a person overcoming adversity and turning their life around. I witnessed how someone can show up in any and every situation, going from the very top to the bottom and climbing back up again. I'll forever be grateful to

Mike for trusting me to work with him. To be a part of his journey when he signed with the Pittsburgh Steelers when no one knew he would have another opportunity to play meaningful snaps as a quarterback in the NFL.

Being around Mike gave me a beautiful example of how healing forgiveness is. Mike has a heart of gold. He's an outstanding human being. In the same way that I could forgive my mom and forgive myself, I can see how much Mike has received forgiveness in his life. When we decide to forgive, we take the weight off ourselves. When we forgive, we're no longer carrying any baggage and letting that stress stop us from living out our dream and being the best version of ourselves.

This process is taught to, and experienced by, all my clients. In phase one, we thoroughly layout all the places where the person feels angry, resentful, mad, judgmental, or similar feelings. We take the time to deeply explore them, unpack all the nuances of the specific situation, make a list of all the stories and thoughts that are not serving them, write it down, then if they feel called to, they burn that list away.

This has been found to have a very cathartic effect for each client. This forms an astonishing amount of lightness in the body. One can feel energy become unstuck and flow through the body as it's supposed to. There are very few feelings that I have experienced that are as powerful as this. Forgiveness is the catalyst to this process. It has been and continues to be the most impactful tool in my arsenal. I'm confident that anyone who has gone through this process will agree.

What You Can Stop Doing

Stop thinking that forgiveness benefits the other person/people involved.

 ### What You Can Start Doing

Realize that the benefits of forgiveness are for you.

 ### How You Can 2

Decide to forgive anyone you are currently holding resentment for. Understand that by ignoring this person or people, you are releasing a massive burden off yourself. Once you forgive, check-in on how you feel. If you still feel the heavy burden, re-evaluate where you still hold resentment and do the process again until you know you have truly forgiven.

Chapter 12: Life Is Now

"You must live in the present, launch yourself on every wave, find your eternity in each moment. Fools stand on their island of opportunities and look toward another land. There is no other land; there is no other life but this."
- Henry David Thoreau

We were four weeks into my mom being in her coma after her unsuccessful surgery to remove the excess skin from her midsection and repair her hernia. For the past four weeks, she was hooked up to all kinds of machines and cables, reminiscent of something you would see on the ER TV show. She was on a ventilator, which was inserted into her throat to help her breathe and keep her alive. She was not able to communicate verbally with any of us. Every time I visited her at the special care hospital, I would see her fidgeting in so much pain, yet she would not be able to tell anyone what was wrong. She had no way of communicating with the doctors and nurses working with her or her family who came to visit.

There was one specific day at the hospital that I will remember for the rest of my life. My brother, my uncle, Scott, and I traveled together to see my mom. We each took our turns to have our one-on-one time with her. I walked into the cold, dark room, turned to my left, and saw my mom laying in her bed with barely any life left in her. Upon seeing her, I walked up to her large hospital bed, came up close to her, touched her cold hand, and looked down at her pale, white face.

This was not the first time I went to visit my mom in this condition. At first, I would visit her a few times a week. In my previous visits, she seemed lifeless. Her eyes would be open, but it would seem as though she was staring off into the distance. She was not there. There was no connection. However, this day was different. This was the first time we were able to make eye contact since our argument the day before her surgery. Within my soul, I could feel that my mom was there and that she knew that it was me standing in front of her.

I'll never forget the immense amount of pain I saw in her eyes that day. Her brown eyes were welling up, getting watery, and became glassy. My mom and I always had a powerful connection, and we could feel what each other were experiencing. Deep down, I could feel that she could not believe that she was in this daunting predicament. She could not believe that she was laying in what would be her death bed. She had many health scares in her past that led to days and sometimes weeks spent in the hospital, but none of those situations felt like this one. Sadly, this had a feeling of finality to it. These were the thoughts and feelings that ran through me as we stared into each other's eyes.

Even from her position in that hospital bed, she could tell that I was in deep mental and emotional agony. After a few moments together, I began crying harder than I've ever cried in my entire life. A wave of shame filled my entire body as I told her how sorry I was for how I treated her. All I could think of were the fights that I started, the arguments we had, the way I isolated myself from her, my lack of appreciation for her, and all the other horrible ways I treated her. This was the first time that I truly comprehended the hell I put her through the last four years of her life.

I poured my heart out to my mom because this was the first time she was cognitively there since we had our final argument the day before she went into her surgery. This was my chance to express all my regrets fully. Every single piece of sorrow, guilt, and shame within me was shared. A huge part of me did not want to admit it at the time, but I knew that she would not make it out of that hospital. This was my last chance to express how awful I felt and let her know how sorry I was before she was physically gone forever.

The main point I desired to express to my mom was how much I loved her. It took my mom being on her death bed for me to realize how much I withheld my love from her for all these years. My lack of gratitude, compassion, and love showed through my anger, silence, and withdrawal. This all hit me like a ton of bricks when I realized that I would never have a relationship with my mom again. We were never going to have the opportunity to laugh together. There were no more opportunities to have deep conversations about life. She was never going to be able to tell me how much she loved me. I was never going to be able to give her those big bear hugs that I had given her since I was a little boy. She would never see me get married or be able to play with her grandchildren. In those last moments at her bedside, I did my best to tell her how much she meant to me in that moment and throughout my entire life.

After pouring out all my feelings and emotions, feeling empty, I left my mom's side. The lonely walk down the stairs felt like miles before I reached the exit of the hospital. I sadly sat in my car in the hospital parking lot for hours. Both of my hands and my forehead were planted on the steering wheel, wondering to myself, "How the fuck did I get here?" A mix of confusion, misery, and shame filled every cell of my body. Here I was, thinking that my life was operating at a high level. However, sitting in my car, I realized that this wasn't the case at all. I was living as a shell of myself, taking my life and the lives of those I love for granted.

With my forehead on the steering wheel, I made a promise to myself. From that point on, I was going all in on life. Knowing that my mom would die and that I would never have the opportunity to be with her again moved the cliché of "life is now" from something I heard, to something I understood. There's no time to waste. Before this moment in my car, I consistently put things off regarding myself, my family, and my career endeavors. I was living in tomorrow, thinking that anything could wait until the next day. That was my biggest mistake.

The lesson of this mistake had me shift my life to living in the moment. With a new awareness of how fragile and uncertain life can be, I prioritized being present. To focus on the here and now intentionally. This lit the fire in me to begin focusing on the things I could control. It ended up catalyzing my personal growth. I started to put in more and more work on myself. This showed up in the form of investing in my human potential coaching certification, investing in my life coach, attending seminars and training, reading dozens of personal development books, and listening to podcasts geared towards personal mastery.

Most importantly, I embodied and applied all that I learned. My life immediately leveled up. By understanding that life is now, I took it upon myself to urgently apply my new knowledge to my personal life, relationships, and career. This new practice of immediate application allowed me to grow and accomplish new feats. Being present allowed me to embrace these new accomplishments and truly feel gratitude for what I created.

If I did not take the time to realize that life is now and practice presence, I would have continued to live my life in such a way where nothing I did was good enough. I would have easily continued down the path of underestimating myself, playing small, and thinking I was unworthy of greatness. Living the mantra "life is now" enables me to celebrate my wins and use them as evidence that all my trials and tribulations with my mom did not happen in vain.

My mom and our relationship played a tremendous role in being a Georgetown graduate, a former Division, I football player, changing my life for the better, and helping so many other people do the same. In my professional career, I had the opportunity to train elite athletes like Michael Vick, Chris Chambers, Wes Welker, Kevin Burnett, Lousaka Polite, Jeff Conine, Manny Ramirez, Luis Castillo, Alex Gonzalez, Neville Hewitt, Lafayette Pitts, Ray-Ray Armstrong, K'Waun Williams, Alex Erickson, Quenton Dunbar, Darryl Roberts, Bobby Hart, Yakhouba Diawra, Sonya Kenin and Genie Bouchard, to name a few.

I started working with partners from large international law firms, executives, entrepreneurs, and other high performers outside of professional sports. This allowed me to work with people who are already some of the best in their respected fields to develop holistic lives, impacting their careers and every aspect of their lives. Teaching them how to prioritize their awareness, optimize their health, and actualize their potential to maximize their lives. We developed foundational health principles on properly eating, hydrating, sleeping, thinking, breathing, and moving. My focus is on co-creating unique, sustainable systems for their long-term growth and development. What fulfills me most is that they have achieved great success and know how to create that success and fulfillment on their own.

I'm so grateful that I can empower people to live all in and create their dream life. Dream life is a life where every pillar of fulfillment gets the love and attention it requires. This includes, but is not limited to one's career/finances, health/wellness/fitness, personal relationship with their partner, relationships with their friends and family, personal growth, spiritual growth, leisure, and ultimately, how they build and contribute to the community at large. To be able to help people level up these aspects of life brings me great joy. I can help others in this way because I make it a priority to work on these pillars in my own life. While my mom's death caused me so much pain, it also catalyzed the work I have put in to better myself and apply this work with my clients.

Through my history and work with my clients, it's now apparent that there's no reason to wait to improve our lives. Life is now. This means that it takes a conscious decision to get clear on where you currently are in your life, where you desire to be, and what is getting in the way. This requires a great deal of introspection, honesty, compassion, and self-love.

It's common to be self-critical and beat yourself up for not being where you think you are "supposed to be in life." But that typically isn't effective. What is compelling is committing to being your best self and understanding that that is accomplished by focusing on what you can do at this moment. What is the first action you get to take to change for the better? What can you do right now at this moment to advance in the direction you desire to go? Who can you talk to? Who can mentor you? Who can help you create more clarity so that you can take committed action? Why is all of this important? Asking yourself these types of questions can provide you with the answers required to improve and level up. No one can do it for you. You also don't have to do it alone. Do it because you matter. Do it because you are worth it.

I know what it is like to feel unworthy. I know what it is like to feel lost and confused. I know what it is like to feel shame, guilt, and sorrow. What I also know is how to overcome these ineffective ways of thinking and to be. The key is to realize that life is now. There is no time to wait. The best time to start was years ago. The second-best time to start is this moment.

My mom's untimely death was the turning point in my life. May 14, 2015, was the day my mom left this Earth. It was also the day that my transformation began. Losing my mom in this fashion made me re-evaluate how I was living my life. I couldn't have imagined this at the time, but the way she died and where our relationship was at the time turned me into the man that I am today. I easily could have crumbled when my mom died. I could have adopted a victim mentality and allowed my life to spiral.

Fortunately, something deep within me had me look in the mirror and take ownership of my situation. It allowed me to look inwards, find what was not working, and decide to do better. My outlook on life changed. My goals changed. My actions changed. This resulted in the next seven years of my life, up to the writing of this book being the best seven years of my life. My physical, emotional, mental, and spiritual health are the best they've ever been. I love the work I do. I'm blessed to have amazing relationships with my fiancé, friends, and family. I'm grateful to continually work on my personal and spiritual growth, engage in activities I love, and to be building a tremendous community around me.

This is all available to you as well. Every single goal that you want to achieve requires your direct love, attention, and committed action. When you put in the work, everything is possible. We see it happen around us every single day. Take a moment to think about your main goal in life or the biggest change you would like to create. Who do you know personally or have you seen out there who has accomplished the same goal or something similar? How did he do it? What worked for her? There is somebody out there just like you who achieves the exact type of results you're trying to achieve. Please understand that if they can do it, then YouCan2.

 ### What You Can Stop Doing

Stop waiting to do the things that matter to you in life. Stop thinking that you have until tomorrow, next week, next month, or next year to go after the things you love or tell those closest to you that you love them.

 ### What You Can Start Doing

Be present! Treat your priorities as such. Take massive action now! CREATE! CREATE! CREATE!

 ### How You Can 2

If there is someone that you want to talk to, do it now. If there is a place you desire to visit, book it now. If there are projects that are important to you, work on them daily. You are a powerful creator. Anything that you want to accomplish gets to be worked on NOW.

Fin

Glossary

Ayahuasca: Ayahuasca is a South American (pan-Amazonian) psychoactive brew used both socially and as ceremonial spiritual medicine among the indigenous peoples of the Amazon basin

Backfield: The area of play behind the offensive line

Comfort Zone: The level at which one functions with ease and familiarity

Compassion: Understanding that someone else does not understand

Dream Life: The life experienced when an individual is living in alignment with their values and are giving love and attention to all domains of their life; A life where one is consistently operating at their best

Emotional Intelligence: Your ability to recognize, understand, and manage your own emotions

Emotional Resilience: Your ability to adapt to stressful situations or crisis

Experiential Learning: The process of learning through experience and is more narrowly defined as "learning through reflection on doing"

Mesa: A portable alter holding personal power objects that afford a microcosm of the universe for healing and ritual.

Nutrient dense: Having high vitamin and mineral content related to its weight

Open field: Any area in the playing field away from the heavily trafficked line of scrimmage

Psylocibin: A naturally occurring psychedelic prodrug compound produced by more than 200 species of fungi.

Sack: Occurs when the quarterback is tackled behind the line of scrimmage before he can throw a forward pass

Tackle for loss: A tackle behind the line of scrimmage resulting in lost yardage

TRX: A specialized form of suspension training equipment

Visceral: Relating to deep feelings as opposed to intellect

#90 Alvey Thompson, Jr

Georgetown University Football

Made in United States
Orlando, FL
01 January 2022

12767048R00080